LEVEL CRIMSON

MCIComprehension

STUDENT EDITION

Making Connections® Reading Comprehension

EDUCATORS PUBLISHING SERVICE
Cambridge and Toronto

Contents

Unit 4: Literary Devices ◆ It's All a Mystery

Unit 5: Recognizing Viewpoint: Author's Perspective ◆ Disaster!

Unit 6: Synthesizing Information ◆ Intriguing Investigations

Be an Active Reader

We want you to write in this book! Marking the text helps you...

- remember what you've read
- understand what you've read
- answer questions about what you've read

As you read the texts in this book, you will

1. **mark for meaning** by circling words and phrases you can't read, or can read but don't understand. You will learn vocabulary strategies to help you figure these out.
2. **mark for skills** by underlining examples of the skills you are learning. The skills in this book are

- compare and contrast
- cause and effect
- making inferences
- literary devices
- recognizing author's perspective
- synthesizing information

Below is an example of a marked text. This reader circled words and phrases she found difficult. Then she underlined causes in blue and effects in green.

Young Frederick was born in 1818 as Frederick Bailey. His mother, an enslaved person on a farm in Maryland, worked long, hard hours. As a result, Frederick was raised by his grandmother, who lived in a cabin near the farm.

ATHLETIC ADVENTURES

- 🎾 *Two teams battle it out on the basketball court. Which one keeps its cool to win the game?*

- 🎾 *One could barely walk. The other lost her leg. How did two world-class athletes overcome the odds to succeed?*

- 🎾 *It's an ancient sport versus a modern one. Which one turns deadly in the end?*

Unit 1

Compare and Contrast To compare and contrast, identify how things are similar and how they are different.

SPRINGFIELD HIGH SCHOOL ★ SENTINEL
★ FEBRUARY 8, 2008 ★

BEARS LOSE

What makes a matchup between these two teams so exciting?

Fairview Wildcats Roar to Victory
by Simone Reardon

Bears fans are still reeling from yesterday's loss at Springfield High. The Springfield Bears fell 67–66 to their rivals, the Fairview Wildcats, in an epic basketball game. The Bears jumped to a big lead in the first half, but the Wildcats stormed back to win it in the end.

This was the two teams' second meeting this season. The Bears won the first game 85–84 in overtime. The rivalry between the Springfield Bears and the Fairview Wildcats is longstanding. Every game between them goes down to the wire, and yesterday's game was no exception. Here's a quarter-by-quarter recap of the heartbreaking loss.

First Quarter

It was a very low-scoring first quarter. Neither team played very well as both teams missed a number of wide-open shots. "It seemed like the teams were feeling each other out in the first quarter," said longtime Bears fan Maria Fleming. "They were trying to establish their very different playing styles."

The Bears went with a faster, more aggressive style of play. Several times, they were able to break free of Wildcats defenders and score some easy baskets. The Wildcats, on the other hand, tried to slow the game down with their defense. They were able to block several shots and even steal the ball out of their opponents' hands. Both styles worked equally well at first, and after one quarter the game was tied 12–12.

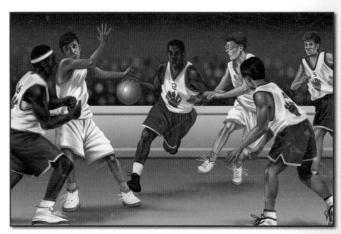

The Bears started the game with an aggressive style of play.

Second Quarter

The Bears exploded for 26 points in the second quarter, and Bears star player Nick Simms had 21 of those points. "Every time I got the ball, I knew I was going to make the shot," said Simms. He went nine for nine from the field and also made three free throws.

Simms was a star player for the Bears.

"We just couldn't stop him," said Wildcats Coach Alison Brown. "It was a rough second quarter for us." But Brown and her players didn't panic. Brown never lost her cool, and her attitude kept her players positive.

As Bears fans know, Coach Vince Hill has a very different coaching style. He is known for pacing the sidelines like a madman and yelling at his players if they do something wrong.

Both coaching styles seemed to be effective, however. No matter what the score was, every player on the court stayed focused and played hard. After two quarters, the Bears led 38–22.

Third Quarter

Coach Brown brought in a new game plan for the third quarter—the Wildcats would stop Nick Simms at all costs. Coach Brown made sure three players were guarding Simms every time he had the ball, making it impossible for him to shoot. Simms had to pass to his teammates, who had trouble making baskets.

The Bears players made only three out of ten shots in the third quarter. "We were just awful in the third quarter!" said Coach Hill after the game. "We can't rely on just one player! If any of those guys had made some shots in the third quarter, we might have won."

While the Bears struggled, the Wildcats began sinking shot after shot. Unlike the Bears, the Wildcats do not have a superstar. They do have several solid players who score in game after game, and just about every player on the Wildcats scored during the third quarter. The team scored 20 points while the Bears only scored 6. At the end of the third quarter, the Bears still led 44–42, but they were hanging on by a thread. CONTINUED…

The captains of the Bears and the Wildcats shake hands after a tough game.

Fourth Quarter

The Bears bounced back in the fourth quarter. The Wildcats had to give up guarding just Simms when other Bears players finally began making shots. "We were leaving the other guys too wide open, and we had to guard them more," said Wildcats player Darius Lincoln. With more opportunities to shoot, Simms caught fire and tied the score 61–61 with five minutes to go.

At that point, the two teams played with more intensity than ever. Both the Bears and Wildcats players were giving it everything they had. With the score tied 65–65 and with thirty seconds to go, the Wildcats had the ball and took their time to find an opening. Then Lincoln took the ball and lobbed a three-pointer. He didn't make it, but he grabbed the rebound and dunked it in, putting the Wildcats ahead 67–65.

When the Bears got the ball back, there were only ten seconds left, and Simms had the ball in the final possession. As he went to take a shot, he was fouled with one second to play. If he made both free throws, the Bears would send the game to overtime. He made the first shot easily, but his second shot bounced off the backboard, rolled around the rim, and fell to the floor. The Wildcats grabbed the rebound as time expired. Lincoln threw the ball into the air in victory, and the Wildcats went away with a hard-fought win.

"The Wildcats were the better team tonight," said Coach Hill.

"That was the toughest game we've played all season!" said Coach Brown. "I have a feeling we'll be seeing them again in the playoffs."

Brown could be right. With the playoffs only a month away, there is a probable rematch in the near future. That isn't much comfort to Bears fans right now, though. A loss like this could sting for a while. ■

Practice the Skill

Compare and Contrast

Fill in the Venn diagram. How were the two teams similar in the first two quarters? How were they different?

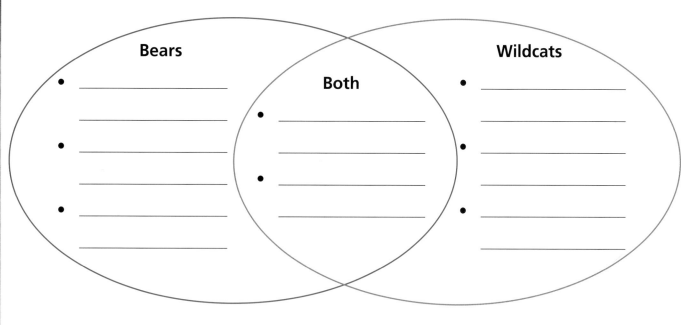

Check Comprehension

1. Why did the Bears have trouble scoring in the third quarter?

   _____

   _____

2. Why did Simms do so well in the fourth quarter?

   _____

   _____

Vocabulary

Write the sentence from page 8 that tells what *intensity* means.

_____

_____

RUNNING WITH COURAGE

How are the struggles of these two athletes similar? How are they different?

Wilma Rudolph is remembered as one of the United States' greatest athletes, and in her time, she was called the fastest woman in the world. When she was a young girl, though, she could barely even walk.

April Holmes is another great athlete. She has set several world running records, and she has done all this after losing part of her leg in an accident.

Professional athletes go through many struggles to reach the top, but few athletes have struggled more than Wilma and April. Their paths to greatness took strength, courage, and determination.

Wilma Rudolph

Illness and Injury

Wilma and April took very different roads to become great athletes. Wilma was born on June 23, 1940, in Clarksville, Tennessee. She had a difficult childhood right from the start, suffering from many illnesses. She endured measles, mumps, scarlet fever, chicken pox, pneumonia, and polio. Every one of them could have killed her. Even though she was sick so much of the time, Wilma's hospital aid was limited. In Tennessee in the 1940s, African Americans were not allowed to attend the best local hospitals. But Wilma did not give up. She fought for her life and survived every single illness.

April Holmes

But Wilma did not escape unharmed, and as a result of one of her illnesses, she lost movement in her left leg. The doctors fit her with a metal brace to help her move around, but even with the brace, Wilma moved very slowly. Doctors doubted that she would ever walk normally on her left leg.

April, on the other hand, was perfectly healthy growing up. She was born on March 11, 1973, in Hopedale, New Jersey. April showed great promise as an athlete, and in high school, she was a champion in the 400-meter race. She then won several track-and-field events during her college career.

Then in 2001, disaster struck. April was trying to board a train in Philadelphia, but she fell onto the track. A passing train couldn't stop in time and ran over April's left leg. It took rescuers thirty minutes to free her from the tracks. That night in the hospital, the doctors had to cut off her left leg just below the knee. Just like with Wilma, doctors didn't know if April would ever walk on her left leg again.

Persistence Pays Off

Wilma didn't let setbacks stand in her way. She found a hospital in Nashville where doctors were willing to treat her leg. The hospital was forty-five miles from her house, but Wilma's mother drove her daughter there every week. She received treatment and was shown some exercises to do at home. She did the exercises every day. Her brothers and sisters also helped by massaging her leg to help her regain feeling in it.

Wilma's brace came off when she was nine and was replaced with a special shoe. When she was eleven, she no longer even needed the shoe. As a young girl, she had always wanted to play basketball with her brothers and sisters, and finally, her dream became a reality.

April showed just as much courage and willpower in her struggle to walk again. The doctors fitted her with a prosthetic leg after four months in the hospital. As she recovered, she read several magazines about disabled athletes competing in races. These stories inspired April and drove her to recover. She began walking on her new leg just six months after her accident, and she began running on it one month after that.

April's prosthetic leg

A Race to the Top

Wilma and April both showed great promise soon after they recovered. When she was sixteen, Wilma competed at the 1956 Olympics in Melbourne, Australia, where she won a bronze medal for the 4 x 100-meter relay. While a less determined athlete might be pleased with third place, Wilma was not. She returned to Tennessee and enrolled at the state university, where she trained hard for the 1960 Olympics in Rome, Italy.

April's story is similar to Wilma's. In 2002, she began taking part in races for people with disabilities. She finished second in the 100-meter dash at a World Championship race in France and set a United States record. But just like Wilma, April wouldn't settle for anything but first place. She started training for the biggest event in disabled sports, the Paralympics.

April Holmes at the 2004 Paralympics

Champion Runners

Wilma finally achieved her goal at the 1960 Olympics, when she won her first gold medal in the 100-meter dash, and then another in the 200-meter dash. She wanted her third gold in the 4 x 100-meter relay, the race she had won a bronze medal in four years earlier.

Four teammates race in the 4 x 100-meter relay. Each team member runs 100 meters. Wilma ran last, when victory seemed impossible. But with her teammates cheering, Wilma managed to pass the other runners just before the finish line. She became the first American woman to win three Olympic gold medals in track and field events.

Wilma Rudolph winning gold at the 1960 Olympics

April has not won a gold medal yet, but she has come close. At the 2004 Paralympics, she set a world record in both the 100-meter and 200-meter dashes and also won a bronze medal in the long jump competition. Today, April is considered one of the fastest athletes in disabled sports.

Off the Track

Both Wilma and April are known for more than just their athletic abilities. Their inspiring work has made a difference in many people's lives.

April Holmes competing in the long jump at the 2004 Paralympics

Wilma received many honors for her achievements in Rome, but she never competed at the Olympics again. Instead, she retired from racing to start a family, while also taking a job as a teacher and track coach. In her spare time, she took on many noble causes. One of her goals was to end laws that discriminated against African Americans. Wilma's determination paid off when the protest marches she took part in helped rid Tennessee of these laws. Sadly, Wilma died of cancer in 1994.

April has not retired from racing yet, but that doesn't stop her from doing great work. She often goes to hospitals to visit other people who have lost limbs, telling them her story and giving them hope. Her charity, The April Holmes Foundation, gives people with disabilities the equipment they need to become as active as she is.

There have been many great female athletes over the years. However, few can match the courage, determination, and heart of Wilma Rudolph and April Holmes. Their amazing feats on and off the track will always be remembered.

Practice the Skill

Compare and Contrast

Look on pages 10–11 to complete the Venn diagram. Compare and contrast Wilma and April's lives.

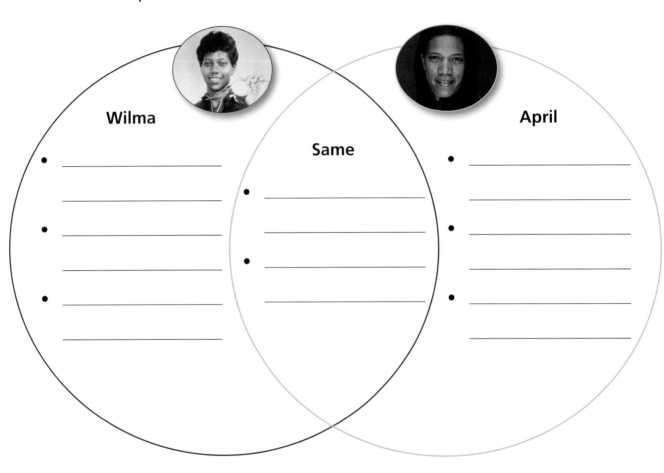

Wilma

April

Same

Check Comprehension

1. What was Wilma's dream as a young girl?

   _____

   _____

2. As April recovered, she read magazines about disabled athletes. What effect did this have on her?

   _____

   _____

Going for the Gold

Look on pages 12–13 to answer these questions.

1. The text describes two champion runners with some different accomplishments. Write either **Wilma** or **April** to answer each question.

Who trained at Tennessee State University?	
Who competed in the 2004 Paralympics?	
Who won a gold medal in the 4 x 100-meter relay?	
Who won a bronze medal in the long jump?	

2. How is April's life outside of racing similar to Wilma's?

_____

_____

Vocabulary

Write the meaning of each word as it is used in the text.

• willpower (page 11) _____

_____

• feats (page 13) _____

_____

Writing

Which athlete do you think had a more difficult struggle? Explain why you think so.

Pok-ta-Pok
Versus SOCCER

In what ways is a pok-ta-pok court different from a soccer field?

If you traveled back in time about three thousand years, you might see the ancient Maya playing a game called pok-ta-pok. The game involved two teams passing a ball back and forth without using their hands. The Maya world, in what is now Mexico and Central America, was full of pok-ta-pok fans. In fact, the Aztecs, Olmecs, and other ancient cultures played versions of the game as well. It seems to have been the most popular sport of ancient Central America.

If you think pok-ta-pok sounds a little bit like soccer, you are not alone. Many historians like to compare the two. While there are some similarities between these games, there are also differences.

Rules of the Game

It is hard to compare these two games because the rules of pok-ta-pok were never written down. But archaeologists have pieced together some of the rules by studying Maya ruins and artifacts.

A stone hoop on a pok-ta-pok court

The aim of pok-ta-pok seems to have been to keep the ball in the air and not let it hit the ground. The ball was probably passed from a player on one team to a player on the other team. If a player let the ball hit the ground, the other team would receive points. This is very different from soccer, where the ball can hit the ground and is passed to other teammates, not opponents.

Like soccer players, pok-ta-pok players had a way to score goals. Archaeologists have found stone hoops attached to either side of some of the pok-ta-pok courts. These hoops were just big enough for a pok-ta-pok ball to pass through. It is believed that if a player hit the ball through one of the hoops, that player's team automatically won the game.

The Game Ball

Soccer balls are made of leather and filled with air. Pok-ta-pok balls, on the other hand, were made of solid rubber. To make them, the Maya mixed the juice of a Morning Glory vine with the sap of a rubber tree. The result was a hard mass of rubber, which they shaped into a ball.

Pok-ta-pok balls were far more dangerous than soccer balls. A fully inflated soccer ball weighs about one pound. Pok-ta-pok balls weighed about eight pounds. In soccer, players bounce balls off their heads all the time. If someone tried to do that with a pok-ta-pok ball, they could get seriously injured—even killed—if they hit it hard enough.

Safety Gear

Soccer players typically wear shin guards and mouth guards. This safety gear prevents injuries from the ball or other players' kicks.

With an eight-pound ball coming at them, pok-ta-pok players needed more protection than soccer players. They wore arm guards, knee guards, and sometimes masks and helmets. They also wore a piece of equipment around their waist called a yoke.

The yokes were made of cloth, leather, and wood. They offered more than just protection—they were also important tools for scoring. As in soccer, pok-ta-pok players couldn't use their hands to pass the ball. They also couldn't use their feet. To make up for this, they used their arms, knees, hips, and other body parts to hit the ball. It is believed that players most often tried to bounce the ball off their hips. This would be very painful without a yoke!

This ancient sculpture shows a pok-ta-pok player wearing safety gear.

The Field of Play

Soccer is typically played on a flat, grassy field. Pok-ta-pok was played on a flat, stone court. The pok-ta-pok court was about the same width as a soccer field, but only about a third as long. Unlike soccer's rectangular playing field, the pok-ta-pok court was shaped like the capital letter I.

The biggest difference is that the pok-ta-pok court had walls. These walls were slanted at the bottom so that players could bounce the ball off them without letting it hit the ground. The stone hoops were sometimes attached to the walls. Fans could sit along the top of these walls to watch the games.

Pok-ta-pok courts were shaped like an I.

Entertainment

Entertainment is usually offered before a soccer game or during halftime. The same was true for pok-ta-pok. Musical instruments found at the ruins of pok-ta-pok courts means there was probably live music at the games.

Maya sculptures of the pok-ta-pok courts show drummers seated on pedestals and facing the field. The drummers could have been part of the entertainment, or they may have been part of the game itself. Some historians think the drums acted as a kind of signal to the players.

Popularity

Few sports can match the popularity of soccer. It is the number one sport in countries all over Europe, South America, and Africa. Every four years, teams from thirty-two countries throughout the world compete in a soccer tournament called the World Cup. The event is watched by millions of people worldwide.

Of course, without television, pok-ta-pok games were watched by far fewer people. Still, pok-ta-pok was immensely popular with the Maya. The Maya were loyal to their teams, and the games were almost certainly well attended.

Importance in Society

In parts of South America and Europe, going to a soccer match is an event not to be missed. One soccer coach even joked that the game was more important than life and death! Yet no matter how important soccer is to some of its fans, it can hardly compare to pok-ta-pok.

Pok-ta-pok games had a very important role among the ancient Maya. Sometimes games were played to celebrate a special event. Other times the games may have been a replacement for war. If two cities were at war, for example, the dispute may have been settled by a game of pok-ta-pok. This would save both cities time, money, and—most importantly—lives.

The game was occasionally a religious event in the Maya community. These games really *were* a matter of life and death. Historians conclude that the losers were probably killed as a sacrifice to the Maya gods. Some members of a *winning* team may also have been offered as sacrifices! The Maya believed sacrifice was necessary for the survival of the community. They thought it pleased their gods and brought their people good fortune.

People today might think aspects of pok-ta-pok are kind of strange. But who knows? In another three thousand years, people may think the same thing about the ancient sport of soccer!

A modern-day soccer field

Practice the Skill

Compare and Contrast

Look on pages 16–17 to complete the Venn diagram. Compare and contrast pok-ta-pok and soccer.

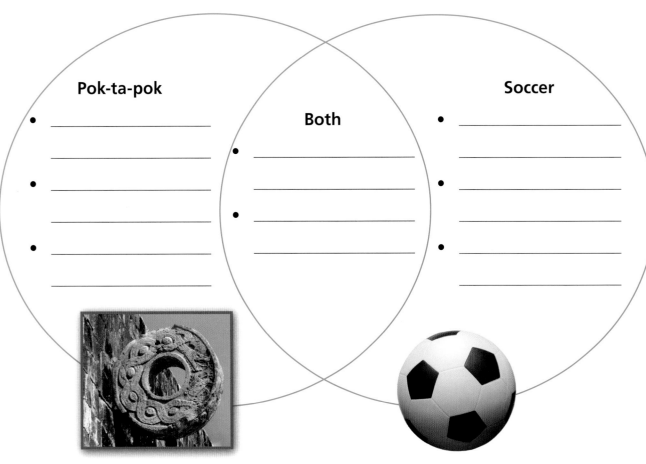

Pok-ta-pok

- _____
  _____
- _____
  _____
- _____
  _____

Both

- _____
  _____
- _____
  _____

Soccer

- _____
  _____
- _____
  _____

Check Comprehension

1. Where did the ancient Maya live?

_____

_____

2. What are yokes? What did the Maya use them for?

_____

_____

A Popularity Contest

Read the facts below. Write either **soccer** or **pok-ta-pok** to tell which sport each fact refers to. If a fact refers to both sports, write **both**.

1. Game watched by millions of people worldwide	
2. Players sometimes killed after losing	
3. Aztecs and Olmecs had own versions of the game	
4. Game used as a substitute for war	
5. Fans passionate about the game	
6. Teams play in tournament called the World Cup	

Vocabulary

1. What is the meaning of *ruins* on page 16?

_____

_____

2. What is the meaning of *sacrifice* on page 19?

_____

_____

Writing

What do you think is the biggest difference between soccer and pok-ta-pok? Explain why you think so.

Text Connections

Now that you have read some texts about athletic adventures, choose one of these activities to explore.

- Write a newspaper article about a sporting event. It can be an event you have seen or one that is made up. Compare and contrast playing styles, coaching, and players of the competing teams.

- Research a great athlete and write a profile about him or her. It can be someone who has retired or someone still competing today. Then exchange your profile with a partner. Discuss the similarities and differences of the athletes you wrote about.

- Research two disabled athletes who compete in the Paralympics. Write a report that compares their stories.

- Find out about another sport played by an ancient culture. Compare and contrast this sport to a sport played today.

- Work with a partner to write a conversation between two people who play different sports. Have each person argue that his or her chosen sport is better.

- Work with a partner or in a small group to invent a new sport. Write instructions on how to play, and include drawings and diagrams.

Continue your explorations by reading these books:

And Nobody Got Hurt! The World's Weirdest, Wackiest True Sports Stories by **Len Berman** Can you believe that a football quarterback once caught his own pass? Read about this and other funny sports stories.

On the Field with . . . Julie Foudy by **Matt Christopher** Julie Foudy is an Olympic soccer champion. How did she get to be so good?

Pacific Crossing by **Gary Soto** How did Lincoln Mendoza get to Japan? It all started with *shorinji kempo* lessons!

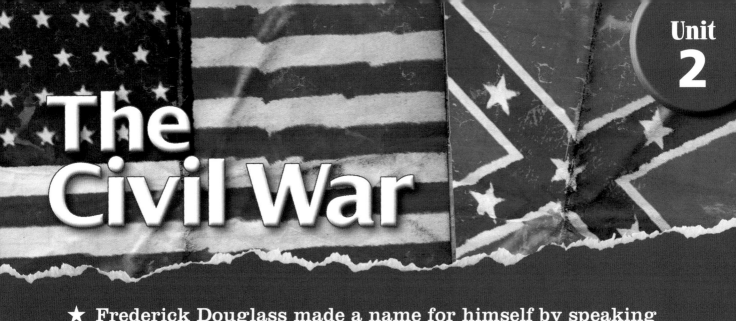

The Civil War

★ Frederick Douglass made a name for himself by speaking out against slavery. How did this escaped slave become one of the most important figures of the Civil War era?

★ Emily Scott's husband died in the Civil War, and she wanted to continue his fight. But could a woman fight in the war?

★ The *Hunley* sank over one hundred years ago. Why did it take so long to find the wreckage?

Unit 2

Cause and Effect   A cause is why something happens, and an effect is the result.

Frederick Douglass: The Fight for Freedom

How did Frederick Douglass become free?

Frederick Douglass was one of the great heroes of the Civil War era, but he did not fight with a rifle. His weapons were his words and his writings. Douglass fought for the rights of African Americans throughout his life, and his work helped put an end to slavery in the United States.

Early Life

Young Frederick was born in 1818 as Frederick Bailey. His mother, an enslaved person on a farm in Maryland, worked long, hard hours. As a result, Frederick was raised by his grandmother, who lived in a cabin near the farm. When Frederick was eight years old, his owner sent him to Baltimore, where he worked as a slave at the Auld estate.

Young Frederick got along well with the estate owner's wife, Sophia. She began teaching Frederick how to read and write. But it was illegal to educate a slave because many people believed that education made slaves more likely to rebel. When Sophia had to stop teaching Frederick, he was crushed. The unfairness and cruelty of slavery made him furious, so he practiced reading and writing on his own and even helped the Aulds' other slaves become literate.

At twenty, Frederick Bailey decided to escape. He was able to obtain papers that said he was a free African American, and he bought a train ticket. No one questioned the papers. When he crossed into the North, where slavery was not permitted, he would be free—unless slave catchers found him. He continued traveling until he reached New York, where he could get lost in the huge city.

Frederick Tells His Story

Frederick Bailey settled in New York and changed his last name to Douglass, which made it harder for slave catchers to track him. As Frederick Douglass, he went to work for the abolitionist movement, a group that aimed to abolish, or end, slavery. He wrote a book called *Narrative of the Life of Frederick Douglass*, which told the story of his life as a slave. It got a lot of attention because many people in the North believed that slaves lived an easy life. Douglass's book showed them the truth, and his story inspired many people to join the abolitionists.

Frederick Douglass speaking in England about his life

Douglass's newfound fame soon became a problem. He worried that the slave catchers would find him. In order to maintain his freedom, Douglass sailed to England. He traveled around the country to speak out against slavery. Douglass's speeches moved many to join his cause. His friends in England even raised enough money to buy Douglass's freedom. In 1846, they paid his former owner $710.96, and at twenty-eight, Douglass was finally free.

Douglass returned to New York and began to lecture across the North. He opened a print shop, began publishing an anti-slavery newspaper, and wrote a second book about his life. Douglass even became involved with the Underground Railroad, a network of people who helped slaves escape to the North.

The War Effort

The Civil War raged through the United States between 1861 and 1865. For Douglass and many others, the war was about slavery. The South wanted to preserve slavery, but the North wanted to abolish it. Douglass became an important figure during the war and even gave advice to President Abraham Lincoln. He also encouraged African Americans to volunteer for the Union army. In fact, Douglass helped form the first African American regiment.

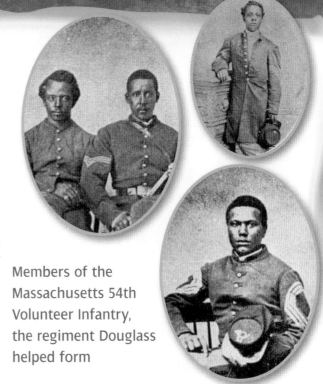

Members of the Massachusetts 54th Volunteer Infantry, the regiment Douglass helped form

Douglass urged African American soldiers to work hard and stand up for their rights. He told them their fight wasn't only against slavery—it was also a fight for U.S. citizenship. Douglass met with Lincoln to talk about the treatment of African American soldiers. He wanted to change the laws so they would get the same pay, treatment, and opportunities as white soldiers.

The Fight for Rights

On April 9, 1865, the Confederate army surrendered. That same year, the Thirteenth Amendment abolished slavery. Douglass was pleased with the amendment, but he realized that African Americans had other problems besides slavery.

President Lincoln was killed five days after the Civil War ended. The following year, Douglass met with the new president, Andrew Johnson. When they talked about voting rights for African Americans, Douglass's arguments impressed Johnson. Four years later, an amendment passed that gave African Americans the right to vote.

Douglass traveled often and spoke about the rights of women and African Americans. He died in 1895, and he is remembered as a great man who fought for the rights of all people.

Practice the Skill

Cause and Effect

Look at the section Frederick Tells His Story. Fill in the chart to show what happened to Frederick.

Cause
Frederick Douglass published *Narrative of the Life of Frederick Douglass.*

Effect
_____
_____

Cause

Effect
_____
_____

Check Comprehension

Besides an end to slavery, what other rights did Douglass fight for?

_____

_____

Vocabulary

Find the word *abolitionist* on page 25. Explain what it means.

_____

_____

Woman in Disguise

THE YEAR IS 1863. THE NORTH AND SOUTH ARE LOCKED IN A BRUTAL CIVIL WAR. BOTH SIDES HAVE SUFFERED GREAT LOSSES SINCE THE WAR BEGAN IN 1861.

IN THE NORTHERN TOWN OF LANCASTER, PENNSYLVANIA, MRS. EMILY SCOTT RECEIVES SOME TRAGIC NEWS.

Dear Mrs. Scott,
We regret to inform you that your husband, Alfred Paul Scott, has been killed in the line of duty. His honorable death in battle was brave and...

EMILY WILL NOT LET HER HUSBAND'S DEATH GO UNANSWERED.

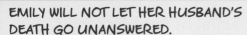

I will take up my husband's fight—I will join the army!

BUT WOMEN AREN'T ALLOWED IN THE ARMY, SO EMILY DISGUISES HERSELF AS A YOUNG MAN.

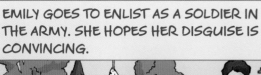

EMILY GOES TO ENLIST AS A SOLDIER IN THE ARMY. SHE HOPES HER DISGUISE IS CONVINCING.

Name?

Frank Johnson.

Can you shoot one of these?

Um, yes...

Best I've seen today, Johnson. Welcome to the army.

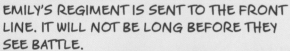

EMILY'S REGIMENT IS SENT TO THE FRONT LINE. IT WILL NOT BE LONG BEFORE THEY SEE BATTLE.

DESPITE THE CLOSE QUARTERS, EMILY KEEPS HER SECRET. IT NEVER OCCURS TO THE OTHERS THAT THERE MIGHT BE A WOMAN AMONG THEM.

THE GENERAL RECOGNIZES EMILY'S IMPORTANT ROLE IN THE BATTLE.

We couldn't have defeated those troops without you, Johnson. Good work!

Thank you, sir. I...oops!

He's a...I mean, she's a...woman!

EMILY CANNOT CONTINUE TO FIGHT AS A SOLDIER, BUT THE ARMY WANTS TO THANK HER FOR HER SERVICE.

Emily Scott, you served the Union well. I hereby give you an honorable discharge.

Thank you, sir.

EMILY ACHIEVES WHAT SHE SET OUT TO ACCOMPLISH.

Alfred, your death was not in vain!

THIS STORY IS BASED ON REAL EVENTS. HUNDREDS—MAYBE EVEN THOUSANDS—OF WOMEN DISGUISED AS MEN JOINED THE ARMY DURING THE CIVIL WAR. THEIR HEROIC DEEDS WILL ALWAYS BE REMEMBERED.

Practice the Skill

Cause and Effect

1. Look at page 28. Write the effect in the box below.

Cause	Effect
Women weren't allowed in the army.	

2. Why is Emily able to keep her secret?

_____

_____

_____

Check Comprehension

1. Why did Emily enlist in the army?

_____

_____

2. Why did the general thank Emily?

_____

_____

The End is Coming

1. Look at page 30. Write the cause in the boxes below.

Cause		Effect
_____ _____ _____	→	The Union wins the battle.

2. How does the army discover that Emily is a woman?

_____

_____

_____

Vocabulary

Define these words as they are used in the text.

- disguises (page 28) _____

- enlist (page 29) _____

- retreat (page 30) _____

Writing

Imagine you are Emily. Write a letter from the front to your family back home.

The Mystery of the *Hunley*

How was the *Hunley* eventually found?

In 1864, a Confederate submarine named the *Hunley* sank a Union ship, the USS *Housatonic*. Then the *Hunley* vanished. No one knows what happened to it.

A City Under Attack

Charleston, South Carolina, was constantly under siege during the Civil War because the Southern city was an important trading post for the Confederacy. The North tried taking control by surrounding Charleston's harbor with ships that blocked delivery ships from bringing in food and supplies. The Confederates needed to end the siege, so in 1863, they began tests on a powerful new submarine, the *H. L. Hunley*. They hoped the submarine was the weapon that would defeat the Union ships.

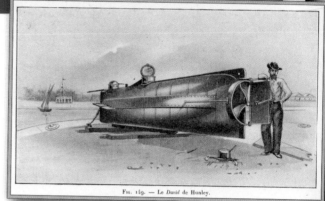

Horace L. Hunley and the submarine he invented

The submarine sank twice during the tests. Many men drowned as a result, including the submarine's inventor, Horace L. Hunley. Some people thought the submarine was too dangerous to use, but others would not give up. They repaired and improved the *Hunley*, and Lieutenant George Dixon took over its command. He trained a new crew to operate it.

The *Hunley* was difficult to maneuver. Crew members worked side by side to turn a long crank by hand. The crank turned a propeller, which moved the submarine. Another crew member steered. The crew had to remember to come to the surface frequently for air. It took several months to prepare the crew for action.

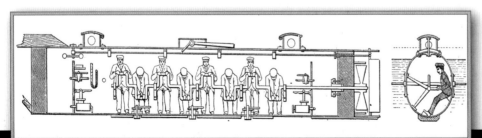

This diagram shows how a crew operated the crank.

One Fateful Night

Finally, Lieutenant Dixon and seven crew members began their journey. They steered the *Hunley* toward a Union ship, the USS *Housatonic*. The *Housatonic* crew sighted the *Hunley* just below the water's surface, but they weren't sure what it was. They knew it wasn't friendly, though. The crew tried aiming their cannons at it, but they couldn't shoot that low into the water. They tried firing their guns at it, but the bullets bounced off the submarine harmlessly.

The *Hunley* crew aimed its torpedo and fired into the side of the *Housatonic*. As the *Hunley* reversed its direction, the torpedo went off and caused a massive explosion on the *Housatonic*. The Union ship sank in just a few minutes.

The USS *Housatonic* under attack by the *Hunley*

With the mission complete, Dixon lit a blue light as a sign of success to men waiting on shore, who added fuel to their signal fires to guide the *Hunley* back. They waited for its return, but the submarine had disappeared into the night.

The Hunt for the *Hunley*

The *Hunley*'s disappearance became a great mystery. Experts suspected the submarine filled with water and the crew drowned. Many people searched the bottom of the harbor for the *Hunley* after the war, and the famous showman P. T. Barnum offered a $100,000 reward for whoever could find the submarine's wreckage. Yet no one could find even a trace of it.

The fate of the *Hunley* remained unknown for more than a century. Then, in 1995, a team of experts set out to find the submarine. Using the latest technology, they found it buried deep in mud at the bottom of the ocean.

Raising the *Hunley*

It took another five years before the diving crew raised the *Hunley*. They had worried the submarine might fall apart if they weren't careful.

First the crew dug the submarine out of the mud, and then they put thirty-two nylon straps underneath it to act as slings and support it. The straps attached to a steel frame that had been placed over the submarine.

The *Hunley* is lifted from the water.

In August of 2000, the *Hunley* was finally ready to rise. A crane hoisted the steel frame, with the *Hunley* inside it, out of the water and onto a barge. After 136 years, the *Hunley* had finally reached the surface. It was taken to a conservation center at the old Charleston Naval Base.

Identifying the Crew

The *Hunley* wreckage was like a gateway to the past. The submarine had filled with silt during its time under water, which helped preserve the crew's remains.

Experts examined the crew's bones and teeth to look for clues. A special type of sculptor recreated the men's faces, which helped experts learn the identities of some of the men. Studying the bones also helped them discover how old the men were when they died.

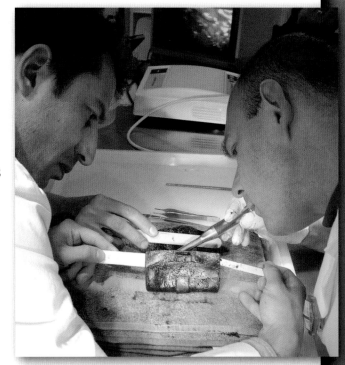

Scientists examine a wallet found on the *Hunley*.

Experts also learned a great deal about the submarine's commander, George Dixon. They found a gold coin engraved with the words "Shiloh April 6, 1862 My Life Preserver G.E.D." near his bones. Supposedly, his sweetheart gave him the coin. When Dixon was shot at the battle of Shiloh, the bullet hit the coin in his pocket, saving his life. From then on, they say, Dixon always carried the coin.

Dixon's gold coin

Unsolved Mysteries

The night the *Hunley* sank remains shrouded in mystery, as the experts still don't know why it sank in the first place. A hole found in its side shows it may have been damaged when the *Housatonic* exploded. It may have also been damaged by gunfire. Of course, the hole may not be a clue at all—something else may have caused the hole long after the submarine sank.

One thing experts know for sure is that the crew members were still positioned at the hand crank when they died. Apparently they had not tried to escape even as the submarine filled with water, which puzzles many people. One theory is that the crew wasn't getting enough fresh air. Maybe they died from a lack of oxygen, not from drowning. The body becomes sleepy when it loses oxygen, so the men may have fallen asleep and let the submarine sink to the bottom of the harbor.

A team of experts continues to look for clues in the *Hunley*. They won't stop until they know exactly what happened, but they hope that modern technology will help provide the answers to this Civil War mystery.

Cause and Effect

Look at the section One Fateful Night. Fill in the chart below.

Cause
The *Hunley* fired a torpedo at the *Housatonic*.

Effect
_____
_____

Cause

Effect
_____
_____

Check Comprehension

1. Why did the Union think it was so important to surround Charleston's harbor with ships?

   _____

   _____

   _____

2. Why were the crew members' remains so well preserved?

   _____

   _____

The Mystery Unravels

1. Look at the section Raising the *Hunley*. Write the cause in the box.

Cause		Effect
_____ _____	→	It took five years of preparation before the diving crew raised the *Hunley* out of the ocean.

2. Explain why the crew may have still been at the hand crank when they died.

   _____

   _____

Vocabulary

1. Find the word *siege* on page 34. Write a sentence using this word.

   _____

   _____

2. Find the word *maneuver* on page 34. Explain what it means.

   _____

Writing

Imagine you are a sailor on a Union ship near the *Housatonic*. Write a description of the *Hunley*'s attack on the *Housatonic*.

Text Connections

Now that you have read several texts about the Civil War, choose one of the following topics to investigate.

★ Work with a partner to research the Underground Railroad. Draw a map of a fictional slave's escape.

★ Read a nonfiction or fictional account of another person who escaped slavery. Compare that person to Frederick Douglass.

★ Emily Scott disguised herself as a man to enlist in the army. Was she right to pretend to be a man in order to achieve her goal? Create two groups and debate the topic.

★ Research the lives of Joan of Arc and Boadicea, two famous female warriors. Draw a timeline of the important events in their lives.

★ Research the *Titanic* or another ship that was located after being under water for many years. Write a report about the ship and what people found.

★ Compare the *Hunley* with the submarines of today. Draw a diagram of a modern submarine and explain how it is different from the *Hunley*.

Continue your explorations by reading these books:

Abner and Me by Dan Gutman
Stosh wanted to know if Abner Doubleday really invented baseball. So how did Stosh wind up in the Battle of Gettysburg?

The Drummer Boy of Vicksburg by G. Clifton Wisler
Orion Howe joins the Union army as a drummer boy. He sees both horrors and heroics on the bloody battlefield.

The Emancipation Proclamation by Ann Heinrichs
When President Lincoln wrote this important document, did he know how it would affect the country?

The Arts in Action

- Keisha's heart is pounding before the big poetry contest. Will the audience cheer her on or will they boo her off the stage?

- A photo assignment leaves Eva feeling less than terrific. Will something change her attitude?

- A gifted artist brings sidewalk drawings to life. How does he do it?

Unit

3

Making Inferences   To make inferences, use what is suggested but not stated directly in a text to better understand characters and events.

A BUNDLE OF NERVES

What does each poem tell about the performers?

I walk into the café, my friend Solana right behind me. I look around the packed room and gasp.

"Look, Keisha, over there," Solana says. She points to a small table in the back. As we push our way through the crowd and grab the table before anyone else can take it, my heart is pounding.

There's a low stage at the front of the room, bare except for a microphone. I can't believe I'll have to stand in that enormous space, where everyone can see me. I look at Solana, shake my head, and say, "There's no way I can go up there."

Suddenly, the stage lights up, and a man wearing a green shirt and a big smile steps onto the stage.

"Hey, how's everyone doing?" he says. The audience claps and cheers.

"I'm your host, Javier, and we've got a great program tonight. But I'm not going to keep yapping—let's get this show moving. Put your hands together for our first poet, Tyrone Martin!"

The room erupts again as Tyrone bounces onto the stage and grabs the microphone from Javier. People shush each other until the room is quiet, and Tyrone finally begins.

You just don't understand me.
It's really such a crime.
Always "be this" or "do that,"
You diss me all the time.
Well, I've got news for you.
You don't have to think I'm cool.
I'm fine with who I am,
And I know how much I rule!

Tyrone struts around the stage, stepping to the beat of his poem as he repeats it. The audience cheers and whistles the second he finishes.

Javier jumps back on stage and says, "Let's hear it for Tyrone!"

When the noise dies down, Javier says, "All right, everyone—let's give it up for our next poet, Megan Porter!"

Megan steps carefully onto the stage without looking at anyone. She stands in the middle of the stage, turns sideways, and hides her face behind her hair. I can hardly hear her at first, and everyone in the audience leans forward to catch her words.

> *Sharp voices snap*
> *Dark eyes burn*
> *Heavy doors slam and echo*
> *Why do they do it?*
> *The same thing every night*
> *They're tearing me apart*
> *Snapping like twigs that crackle in a bonfire*
> *Why do they do it?*
> *They say, "We love you.*
> *It's not your fault."*
> *But those are only words falling softly to the ground*
> *Why do they do it?*
> *I need to show them—*
> *Help them—*
> *Make them see—*
> *We need to stay together.*

We're all quiet for a second, and Megan stands, frozen, on the stage. I like her poem, but I'm not sure how to respond to something so somber. Someone starts to clap, and we all join in, but Megan's applause is quieter than Tyrone's.

"Thank you, Megan," Javier says as he gently helps Megan off the stage. "All right, who's next?" Solana pushes me forward, but my legs turn to jelly, and I can't make them work.

Just then, a group of older guys starts chanting, "Le-o! Le-o! Le-o!" The guy who must be Leo stumbles on stage and starts making up a poem as he goes.

> *Mary had a little lamb.*
> *The little lamb got in a jam.*
> *The big bad wolf helped Mary out.*
> *Now Mary wants to sing and shout.*

The audience boos loudly until Leo leaves the stage. One of his buddies elbows him, and all the guys laugh.

Javier reappears on stage looking confused. "Well, Leo, that was, um, interesting. Anyway, our next poet is Keisha Harold!"

I stand slowly and walk to the stage. The hand holding my poem shakes like a cell phone on vibrate, and I can hardly hear the crowd because my heartbeat is thumping in my ears, as I step carefully onto the stage.

> *This is my city, my crazy city*
> *Feet pounding the pavement*
> *Hiking boots and spiky heels*
> *Through the night*
> *Dark sky overhead*
> *Bright lights, camera, action!*
> *Laughing voices, shouting*
> *Screaming for attention*
> *LOOK AT ME!*
> *People rushing*
> *Cars and buses, bicycles and taxis*
> *OUT OF MY WAY!*
> *People everywhere, like insects*
> *Scurrying, swarming, buzzing.*
> *This is MY city, my crazy city*
> *My frantic, free-spirited city.*
> *NEW YORK!*

The crowd cheers and claps and whistles like crazy! I smile a smile so wide that all my teeth show, and I enjoy the warm spotlight on my face.

Practice the Skill

Making Inferences

Look at the chart below. Use the information to write an inference about how Keisha is feeling.

Information	Inference
• Keisha's heart is pounding. • Keisha gasps when she sees all the people. • Keisha says there's no way she can go up on stage.	_____ _____ _____

Supporting Inferences

Write two pieces of information from the text that support the following inference about Tyrone.

Tyrone is very confident.

• _____

• _____

Check Comprehension

What is Leo and his friends' attitude toward the competition?

_____

Vocabulary

Define each word as it is used in the text.

• somber (page 43) _____

• scurrying (page 44) _____

A SNAPSHOT OF THE CITY

How did Eva, Sharice, and Jerome feel about their new assignment?

Mr. Castillo leaped into the classroom, a huge smile across his face. He carefully placed a large box on his desk and turned toward his class.

"This ought to be good," Eva said to Jerome, rolling her eyes.

"No," said Jerome. "It'll be terrific." *Terrific* was Mr. Castillo's favorite word.

Mr. Castillo cleared his throat and waited for the class to quiet down.

"Terrific, guys, listen up. We're starting a new assignment today," he said, as he pulled out one of the many digital cameras from inside the box. "So here's the deal—you're going to go out and take some *terrific* photos. You'll bring the cameras back here, and we'll print the pictures, okay?" Mr. Castillo paused and the students nodded. "Terrific," he said.

Eva walked to Sharice's place after school. When Sharice opened the door and snapped a picture of her, Eva blinked and asked, "Where's Jerome?"

Sharice shrugged and said, "Wasn't he with you?"

Jerome arrived a few minutes later, out of breath from running. "Sorry, guys," he said, "I just stopped at home to take some photos of my great-grandmother."

"But did you take *terrific* photos?" Eva said, trying to suppress a laugh. "Mr. Castillo wants terrific photos, you know, not photos of some old lady."

"My great-grandmother is not some old lady," Jerome burst out before stopping to glare at Eva. "Well, okay, she's an old lady, but she's really interesting. I got some great—I mean *terrific*—photos."

"I don't think that's what Mr. Castillo had in mind," Eva said.

Sharice cut in with, "Guys, I think we're ready—where should we go first?"

"Let's go wander around outside, see what we find," suggested Jerome.

"That's a dumb idea," said Eva. "This whole assignment is dumb. What kind of terrific pictures does Mr. Castillo think we're going to get, anyway?"

Sharice rolled her eyes. "Come on, Eva. Let's just go."

They walked down the street slowly, looking around for something interesting. Eva randomly took pictures without looking through the viewfinder.

"You're not even trying, Eva," Sharice complained after a few minutes.

Jerome stopped suddenly and said, "Wait a minute—I have an idea." He crouched over and snapped a photo of the crosswalk.

Eva stared, and her jaw dropped open. "What are you doing?" she asked.

"Look at the stripes," Jerome said, pointing. "They make a cool pattern." Then he pointed his camera at a broken curb and pressed the button. After a few more clicks, Jerome had lots of pictures—the legs of pedestrians crossing the street, a shiny red stop sign, and flaky paint peeling off a wall. He even aimed his camera at a thin blade of grass erupting from a crack in the sidewalk.

"Are you crazy?" asked Eva. "This stinks," she said, as she crossed her eyes, stuck out her tongue, and snapped a picture of herself.

They turned the corner, Jerome still clicking away. Sharice looked up at the apartment buildings and stopped, as she pulled on Jerome's arm.

"What?" said Jerome.

Sharice crossed the street and looked back toward them, as she started taking pictures of the buildings. "Look at those terrific curtains!" she said, pointing at the window of a brick building. The curtains inside were olive green with purple stripes.

"Oh, man—curtains?" sighed Eva. "You have *got* to be kidding me."

Sharice kept photographing the apartment buildings, even trying to include a whole row of the rectangular windows in one photograph. "Isn't it neat how they're all the same?" she asked.

Meanwhile, Eva wandered off in search of an ice cream cone. She ordered a cone with two scoops—one chocolate and one strawberry. "Now *this* is what I call terrific," she thought. Eva held the camera at arm's length and snapped a picture of her first lick.

Eva sat down on the ground and happily ate her ice cream cone, as she started taking photos. She caught some pigeons fluffing up their feathers, some leaves swirling in the wind, a street musician, and a puddle. When Eva finished her cone, she headed back to the park to find Jerome and Sharice.

"Did you get some *terrific* pictures?" Jerome asked Eva. "I hope you at least *took* some pictures. It is an assignment, after all."

Eva shrugged and said, "Whatever, I took some."

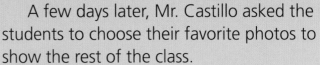

A few days later, Mr. Castillo asked the students to choose their favorite photos to show the rest of the class.

Mr. Castillo printed out the pictures and hung them around the room. There were all kinds of photos—a smiling kid on a swing, a mom hiding from the camera, a statue with a shiny nose, and a dog sitting on an old couch. One person admired Sharice's windows, and someone else liked Jerome's flaky paint. The students agreed that, close up, the paint looked like a skin disease.

Eva glanced toward the end of a row and saw a photo of a dark puddle. The photo was taken at a low angle, so the puddle reflected shadows of light and a white puffy cloud from the sky. Eva wandered over to get a closer look and stared. The cloud looked like a dragon with a pointy tongue and long tail, and the sign under the photo said, "Fire-Breathing Dragon, Eva Ramirez."

Eva was still standing there when Sharice and Jerome came up behind her. "Wow!" Sharice said. "Where'd you take that?"

"I didn't take this," Eva protested. She paused. "Oh, wait—I was eating ice cream," she remembered.

"It's really terrific," Jerome said, with a glance at their teacher.

Mr. Castillo nodded and beamed at them. "It really *is* terrific," he said, before raising his voice to the rest of the class. "Everyone, come look at Eva's photo."

The students gathered around them. "This photograph is all about perspective," he said. "Taken from another angle, it would be just another puddle, and we wouldn't see the dragon at all. But Eva's got a terrific eye."

Eva didn't know what to say, but before she could say anything, Mr. Castillo turned to her.

"Good job, Eva," he said. "You angled the camera in an interesting way, and you included certain background elements that someone else might have left out."

Eva smiled, looking back at her photo. Maybe she *did* have a terrific eye!

Practice the Skill

Making Inferences

1. Read the inference below. Write two pieces of information from the first section of the text that support it.

Information	Inference
• _____ _____ • _____ _____	Mr. Castillo is an enthusiastic teacher.

2. Read the information below. What can you infer about Eva's attitude toward the assignment?

Information	Inference
• Eva said, "This whole assignment is dumb." • Eva randomly took pictures without looking through the viewfinder. • She stuck out her tongue and snapped a picture of herself.	_____ _____ _____

Check Comprehension

1. What is Jerome's attitude toward his great-grandmother?

_____

_____

2. Why does Mr. Castillo say that Eva has a good eye?

_____

_____

After the Assignment

1. Read the inference below. Then write two pieces of information from the text that support it.

Sharice and Jerome deserve a higher grade on the assignment than Eva.
• _____ • _____

2. Do you think Eva will take her next photo assignment seriously? Use information from the text to support your answer.

_____

_____

Vocabulary

Define these words as they are used in the text.

- pedestrian (page 47) _____

- perspective (page 49) _____

Writing

How would you feel if you were given the same assignment? Give reasons for your answer.

Sidewalk Studio

Does a drawing have to be in a frame to be called art? Julian Beever doesn't think so. This English artist creates beautiful images right on the sidewalks of the world's cities. His detailed works can take several days to complete, but they wash away with the next rain.

What is Julian Beever's attitude toward artwork?

Creating an Illusion

Beever's sidewalk drawings are optical illusions. They look like they are three-dimensional—as if his scenes are popping out of the pavement or diving down into it. One drawing shows a woman sunbathing at the beach. Another shows a seal poking its head out of the ice. Some people even walked around Beever's drawing of a pothole because they thought it was really there.

Beever's globe drawing seems to jump right out of the pavement.

From the wrong angle, Beever's globe appears stretched out of shape.

Of course, people are only fooled if they look at the drawings from the correct angle. From the wrong angle, Beever's drawings look distorted, or twisted out of their normal shapes. This type of optical illusion, called anamorphosis, takes advantage of the way our brain interprets the world.

The human brain understands things in a certain way. For example, objects that move toward us seem to grow bigger, and objects that move away from us seem to grow smaller. Anamorphosis plays with these ideas and tricks the brain into thinking a flat, two-dimensional object actually has three dimensions.

How Does It Work?

Beever uses a simple set of tools, including chalk, a sketchpad and pencils, a camera with a wide-angle lens, and a stool.

Beever can't just start drawing and hope for the best. He has to plan the image because he needs to know how the different parts of the image will work together. First Beever decides on a subject and sketches it out on his pad. Then he draws a grid over the sketch to help him transfer the image from the sketchpad to the sidewalk.

The secret to Beever's success is the camera he sets up on a tripod near his work area. As he draws, Beever looks at the image over and over again through the camera's lens. He wants the image to look realistic and three-dimensional from the perspective, or viewpoint, of the camera. By looking at the image through the camera, Beever makes sure he's on track. But that's not all he uses his camera for—Beever also makes sure to take photographs of his finished work.

Drawing on the sidewalk is a lot harder than it looks. Kneeling down and getting up from the ground hundreds of times a day would be difficult for anyone, so Beever always has his stool with him. He rests his stomach on the seat and leans forward, which takes the pressure off his knees and back.

"The secret is to set up a camera on a tripod and keep it in one spot and check every mark you make. It's really just playing with perspective to make it appear different to what it really is."

Julian Beever

One thing Beever doesn't have to worry about is getting cold. The movements required in his work help keep him warm even in cold weather. However, there's little Beever can do if it rains or snows.

Popular Portraits

While Beever is best known for his three-dimensional art, he also draws beautiful portraits. His sidewalk drawing of Princess Diana shortly after her death was seen all over the world. Crowds also gathered to see the portrait that celebrated President Bill Clinton's inauguration.

After more than fifteen years and hundreds of drawings, Beever is sure of one thing. "My art is for anybody. It's for people who wouldn't go into an art gallery," said Beever. "Art shouldn't be locked away in galleries and libraries and books. Art should be for everybody and not just . . . so-called experts."

Crowds gathered to view Beever's portrait of Princess Diana.

Practice the Skill

Making Inferences

1. Read the information below. What can you infer about people's attitudes toward Julian Beever's images?

Information	Inference
• Beever's drawings look three-dimensional. • His scenes look like they are popping out of the pavement.	_____ _____ _____

2. Why do you think Beever takes several photographs of his finished works? Use information from the text to support your answer.

_____

_____

Check Comprehension

1. How does using a grid help Beever with his drawings?

_____

_____

2. Why does Beever think that his art doesn't belong in an art gallery?

_____

_____

Sidewalk Struggles

Read the inference below. Then write two pieces of information from pages 54–55 that support it.

Sidewalk art can be physically demanding.
• _____
_____
• _____
_____

Vocabulary

1. What is *anamorphosis,* and how does it work?

   _____

   _____

   _____

2. Define these words as they are used in the text.

   • distorted (page 53) _____

   • portrait (page 55) _____

Writing

What do you think of Beever's artwork? Explain your thinking.

Text Connections

You have now read several texts about the arts. Choose one of the following options to further explore the arts.

- Research the life of a famous poet. Write a report about how that poet's attitude or ideas are reflected in the poet's works.

- Write a poem about a person you admire. Start by writing the letters of the person's name down the length of a page. Each line of the poem should start with one of these letters. This is called an acrostic poem.

- Find photos of a famous landmark taken from three different angles. Print out, make copies, or draw sketches of the photos. Write captions underneath each one, describing what you like or dislike about the angle used.

- Write a story about Eva's next photo assignment. Be sure to show how her attitude changes from the earlier assignment.

- Write a report about a painting or sculpture that uses optical illusions. Describe the illusion used and how it works.

- Imagine you have been asked to design some artwork to decorate a wall at your school. Create a design that would be suitable for a school wall. Write why you designed this artwork. Share your designs with your classmates.

Continue your explorations by reading these books:

Chasing Vermeer by Blue Balliett
A mysterious thief has stolen a valuable painting. Can Petra and Calder figure out the clues to solve the crime?

Cool Melons—Turn to Frogs! The Life and Poems of Issa, Story and Haiku Translations by Matthew Gollub, illus. Kazuko G. Stone
Discover how Japanese poet Issa wrote haiku to help him through the hard times in his life.

Savion: My Life in Tap by Savion Glover and Bruce Weber
Rap, hip hop—and *tap*? Learn how Savion Glover combined modern music with an old dance to invent something original.

It's All a Mystery

- When Aidan and Jackson go inside the old Tucker house, they get spooked. Who is calling Jackson's name?

- Kyle can't find his new video game. Could one of his friends be the thief?

- Sherlock Holmes is the original crime scene investigator— and he may be the most popular detective who never lived!

Literary Devices   Some literary devices, such as figurative language, create vivid descriptions. Others, such as alliteration and onomatopoeia, use the sound of words for effect.

Campfire Tale

How do the literary devices make this tale spooky?

"So what do we do now?" asked Aidan, as he took a seat around the campfire. Aidan and his friends were on a camping trip with their families at Lazy Loon Lake. They had all just finished eating dinner, and their parents were playing cards by the main tent.

"We could play catch—or even a full game of baseball," Tina suggested, as she reached for her glove.

"I don't think so, Tina. It's too dark outside to see," said Jesse.

"Why don't we tell each other scary stories? That's what people are supposed to do when they sit around a campfire, right?" said Kari.

"I haven't done that in years!" said Tina. "It sounds like fun to me!"

"All right, I'll start—I know a really good one," said Aidan. The four friends huddled in close around the campfire, as Aidan placed a flashlight under his chin. In the dark, the beam from the flashlight turned his face into a mask of terror.

"It all happened one gray, gloomy night last fall, while my buddy Jackson and I were walking home from football practice. We had just passed the old Tucker house on Maple Street. You know those old houses they show in scary movies, with the sloping roofs and the towers and the windows all boarded up? Well, that's just what this house looked like. Nobody had lived in it for at least fifty years . . .

"Anyway, we had just walked past it, when out of nowhere came this huge crash of thunder. Forks of lightning ripped across the sky, followed by a curtain of rain. We ran onto the porch of the Tucker house to take shelter, but the porch didn't offer much protection, and soon we were soaked to the bone. Jackson tried the door, and when it creaked open, he rushed inside."

Suddenly the four friends heard an owl hooting in the distance, and Kari almost jumped out of her skin. "What was that?" she asked.

"It was an owl, you baby!" said Jesse, eager for the story to continue.

"Shh!" said Tina, putting her finger to her lips. "Let him finish the story."

The flickering flames from the fire cast long shadows around the camp. Aidan waited until a hush fell over his audience, then continued.

"I tried to stop Jackson from going in, I really did. I mean, who knows what might have been inside that house? I thought about running away, but I couldn't leave Jackson behind, so instead I went in to find him.

"Inside it was as black as night, and I could only make out some large, bulky shapes lurking in the shadows. Dusty cobwebs twisted around the banisters of the staircase and hung like shrouds from the ceiling.

"I heard muffled sounds coming from the second floor, so I slowly crept up the rotting staircase. The wooden stairs groaned with every step. I was almost at the top when I heard a door swing open and then slam shut. I started to run back downstairs, but something grabbed my shoulder.

"I whirled around and screamed, 'Jackson, don't creep up on me like that! I thought you were—'Suddenly a voice came out of nowhere.

"'*Jack–sonnn!*'

"'Who . . . who's there?' Jackson said. He was shaking like a leaf in the wind, and his face was pale in the gloomy night.

"'*Jack–sonnn!*'

"The voice got louder. 'How does it know my name?' Jackson whispered, as he stared at me, his eyes as wide as saucers.

"'I don't know,' I whispered back, 'but I'm not staying to find out.'

"We stampeded down the stairs—CRASH-THUMP-BANG—and made a dash for the front door. As we sprinted up the street, the sound of footsteps quickened behind us, and then, suddenly, I tripped—"

Tina held her hands to her mouth and cried, "Oh, no, what happened next?"

Aidan started to laugh, and he said, "I looked up and saw Jackson's dad."

"What?" cried the others in surprise.

"Jackson's dad knew we didn't have umbrellas, so he was looking for us along our route home. What we had heard was just Jackson's dad calling his name!"

Kari rolled her eyes, crossed her arms, and said, "That never even happened, did it, Aidan?"

Aidan shrugged, flashed his friends a sly smile, and said, "Maybe it did, and maybe it didn't—but it was scary, wasn't it?"

Jesse grabbed the flashlight from Aidan. "I've heard nursery rhymes scarier than that," he scoffed, as he put the flashlight to his chin.

"Now *this* is a spooky story . . ."

Practice the Skill

Literary Devices

1. The chart below lists examples of figurative language from the text. Write what each one means and what type of figurative language it is.

Figurative Language	Meaning	Type of Figurative Language
The beam from the flashlight turned his face into a mask of terror.		
Dusty cobwebs hung like shrouds from the ceiling.		
The wooden stairs groaned with every step.		
He was shaking like a leaf in the wind.		

2. Write an example of alliteration from the text.

_____

3. Write an example of onomatopoeia from the text.

_____

Check Comprehension

Why did Aidan go upstairs?

_____

Vocabulary

Define these words as they are used in the text.

- route (page 62) _____

- sly (page 62) _____

The Case of the Missing Video Game

> **How do the students use literary devices to show their feelings?**

CHARACTERS:

Kyle	Jin
Maria	Chelsea
Ray	Ms. Garcia
Sam	Other students

SCENE 1

A middle-school soccer field, before school. KYLE, JIN, MARIA, *and* RAY *are playing soccer, and* CHELSEA *is watching. Their backpacks are in a row off to the side.*

CHELSEA: Hey, guys. We should probably get to class. The bell's about to go off.

(The students stop playing, reach for their backpacks, and get ready to go to class. KYLE *and* MARIA *each pick up a blue identical backpack.)*

KYLE: *(proudly patting the side of the backpack)* So I brought the new GameStation Handheld with me today. It's amazing.

MARIA: You're so lucky. I tried getting one last week but they'd already flown off the shelves. How are the graphics?

KYLE: Oh, it's like watching a movie. And the games are so complex. I played *Tomb Invaders* for hours last night, and I'm only on Level Three. You have to be Albert Einstein to figure out some of the puzzles!

RAY: Can I try it some time?

KYLE: Uh, I don't think so. At least not until I beat *Tomb Invaders*.

RAY: C'mon, Kyle, don't be selfish.

(Sound: ding ding ding)

JIN: Man, that bell really beats up your eardrums. C'mon, guys!

(The students exit the stage.)

SCENE 2

> A classroom. KYLE, JIN, MARIA, CHELSEA, RAY, and the other students enter. They place their backpacks on a rack outside the classroom and take their seats. KYLE sits in front of CHELSEA.

KYLE: (*tapping* CHELSEA *on the arm*) Hey, Chelsea, did you hear I got up to Level Three on *Tomb Invaders* last night?

CHELSEA: (*rolling her eyes and turning away*) Good for you. Now go and find someone else to gab to about your goofy game.

KYLE: (*turns back around*) You guys are so jealous.

(MS. GARCIA *enters the room.*)

MS. GARCIA: Good morning, class. Today we're going to learn about the ancient Egyptians. Who can tell us what they already know about ancient Egyptian life?

(RAY *raises his hand.*)

MS. GARCIA: Yes, Ray?

RAY: Is it true that when they made mummies, they removed all the inner organs from the dead bodies?

MS. GARCIA: That's right, Ray. First they dried the organs. Then they wrapped them and placed them in special jars for preservation.

(CHELSEA *raises her hand. Meanwhile,* SAM *enters, gives* MS. GARCIA *a note, and takes his seat.*)

MS. GARCIA: Do you have some more information about the Egyptians, Chelsea?

CHELSEA: No. I just need to go to the girls' room.

MS. GARCIA: Well, you should have gone before class. Be quick!

(CHELSEA *exits the room.*)

MS. GARCIA: Okay, before we get to mummies, I'd like to talk about pyramids.

KYLE: Pyramids? There are pyramids in my new game, *Tomb Invaders*!

(*All the students in the class groan.*)

> The hallway outside the classroom after class. The students are getting their lunches. KYLE opens a small pocket on his backpack. MS. GARCIA is in her classroom reading a book.

KYLE: Where is my GameStation Handheld? I know I put it in this pocket!

(MS. GARCIA rockets into the hallway.)

MS. GARCIA: What's going on out here, Kyle? You're howling like a lost puppy.

KYLE: *(holding up the backpack)* Someone stole my new video game!

MS. GARCIA: *(peering into the backpack)* Are you sure you didn't misplace it?

KYLE: Yes. I know it was stolen. Everyone was jealous of me and wanted it for themselves. *(looks at the students, points to RAY)* It was Ray, I'm sure of it!

RAY: *(shocked)* What?

MS. GARCIA: Why do you think it was Ray?

KYLE: Because I told him I brought it with me to school today.

RAY: So what? That doesn't make me a thief! You told everybody about twenty-two times. You sounded like a broken record.

KYLE: Then it was Sam! He was late for class. He could have grabbed it on the way in.

SAM: *(angry)* C'mon, Kyle! How could I have known you brought it with you if I came in late?

KYLE: Oh, yeah. It must have been Chelsea! She left the classroom. She could have taken it from my backpack and put it in her own.

CHELSEA: You can look in my backpack all you like. It's not there!

(CHELSEA empties her backpack onto the floor. The video game is not there.)

KYLE: Sorry, Chelsea. But *someone* took it!

JIN: Kyle, why don't you check the other pockets of your backpack?

(KYLE opens the other pockets. He holds up a sandwich in a plastic bag and a box of peanuts.)

KYLE: Gross! Tuna fish sandwiches are my worst nightmare! And peanuts make my face blow up like a balloon!

(KYLE holds up a large library book.)

KYLE: What's a boring book about Beijing doing in my backpack?

MARIA: Hey! That's my book! *(snatches the book from KYLE)*

JIN: Which means it's probably *your* backpack, Maria.

KYLE: You mean . . .

JIN: Your backpacks are identical twins. This morning, you must have picked up each other's backpack by mistake.

(MARIA opens the small pocket on a backpack identical to KYLE'S. She pulls out KYLE'S game and waves it in the air.)

MARIA: Here it is! *(hands KYLE the game)*

KYLE: Sorry, everyone. You guys can play my GameStation any time you want.

MS. GARCIA: But not in school! *(takes the game from KYLE)* And next time you can't find it, don't jump to conclusions.

KYLE: Jump? That reminds me of a *Tomb Invaders* level where . . .

(All the students groan.)

Practice the Skill

Literary Devices

1. The chart below lists examples of figurative language from Scene 1. Write what each one means and what type of figurative language it is.

Figurative Language	Meaning	Type of Figurative Language
They'd already flown off the shelves.		
You have to be Albert Einstein to figure out some of the puzzles.		
That bell really beats up your eardrums.		

2. Write an example of onomatopoeia from Scene 1.

_____

Check Comprehension

How does Chelsea prove she's innocent?

_____

_____

Kyle's Clues

1. Kyle uses figurative language to describe the two foods he finds in the backpack. Write both examples below.

_____

_____

2. Write an example of alliteration from Scene 3.

_____

Vocabulary

1. Find the word *preservation* on page 65. Write a sentence using this word.

_____

2. What is the meaning of *identical* on page 67?

_____

_____

Writing

Kyle apologizes at the end of the play, but does he really learn his lesson? Write Scene 4 of the play, and remember to use literary devices.

Sherlock Holmes: CSI

How does the use of literary devices help Sherlock Holmes come alive?

Crime scene investigations are an increasingly popular focus of television shows and movies. Crime scene investigators search the location where the crime occurred for clues. Then they examine the evidence they uncover. Their work keeps us on the edge of our seats.

One classic crime scene investigator is a fictional character named Sherlock Holmes.

Holmes was created in the late 1800s by the English writer Sir Arthur Conan Doyle. Over the next forty years, Doyle wrote four novels and fifty-six stories about his detective. Since then, Sherlock Holmes has become the most famous fictional detective in the world.

A Distinctive Detective

Sherlock Holmes lives in a flat, or apartment, at 221B Baker Street in London, England. How would you recognize him? To start, he is built like a broomstick. He has black eyes and a nose like a hawk.

Holmes's unique clothes also set him apart from the crowd. When he's at work solving crimes, Holmes is often portrayed wearing a long, gray coat and a checked deerstalker hat. A deerstalker hat has four brim flaps. Holmes usually wears the hat with the side flaps tied on top. Another key accessory—the ever-present magnifying glass—defines his familiar appearance.

Sherlock Holmes

Holmes is a famous eccentric. Boxing and sword fighting are two of his hobbies. Music is another, and he is a talented violinist. He also studies chemistry and knows a lot about poisons. Holmes can crack complicated codes and is a magician when it comes to disguises. This variety of interests and hobbies make Holmes an interesting character—and a successful detective.

Some think Holmes wouldn't be half the detective he is without his good friend and trusted assistant, Dr. Watson. Although Watson doesn't have his comrade's eagle eye for detail, he is Holmes's rock. Holmes often relies on Watson to put the pieces of a puzzle together. According to Holmes, "Nothing clears up a case so much as stating it to another person."

Clue Collecting and Thorough Thinking

So how does Holmes even begin to solve a crime? He studies evidence at the scene. For example, he looks at footprints, shoeprints, and even horseshoe prints. He examines the tracks made by carriage wheels and bicycles. Splashes of mud talk to him. They can tell him which part of London the mud—and the bike—came from. Holmes looks closely at a typewritten letter to identify a criminal. He uses a fingerprint to help free an innocent man.

EXAMINING THE EVIDENCE

When Arthur Conan Doyle wrote the Sherlock Holmes mysteries, a new way to solve crimes was developing. Called forensics, it opened a new window into detective work. Forensics involves the use of science in solving a crime.

Forensic investigators are more interested in crime scene evidence than witnesses. Clothes, fingerprints, and DNA speak loudly to them. They might analyze a hair or fiber they find at the scene, or they might measure a shoeprint. They want to answer one important question: does the evidence point to a suspect? In mystery after mystery, Doyle's detail-oriented detective seeks to answer that same question.

But Holmes doesn't rely on physical evidence alone. He also uses logical reasoning to find a solution. For example, it is impossible for one person to be in two places at the same time (unless there are identical twins involved).

Holmes observes the world around him carefully and draws conclusions, or makes deductions, from those observations. If his friend's clothes are damp, he might deduce that the pitter-patter of the rain has wet them. If he sees footprints that are far apart, he might deduce that the person who made them was running, not walking.

Simply put, Holmes uses a variety of techniques to get to the bottom of each mystery. He leaves no stone unturned.

Fans, Films, and Famous Museums

In 1891, Arthur Conan Doyle killed off Sherlock Holmes. His readers were outraged! Doyle had no choice—he brought Holmes back to life for more stories. Even today, Sherlock Holmes has fan clubs all over the world. The names of the fan clubs relate to the Sherlock Holmes stories. The clubs have names like The Six Napoleons of Baltimore and The Keepers of the Bullpup. Club members get together to discuss and promote Doyle's work.

The obsession does not end there. There are over a million Web sites and blogs devoted to Sherlock Holmes. Several countries have issued stamps with his picture on them. And more films have been made about Holmes than about any other book character.

Sir Arthur Conan Doyle

THE HOUND OF THE BASKERVILLES

The Hound of the Baskervilles may be the most famous of the Sherlock Holmes stories. In it, Sir Charles Baskerville has been found dead on his estate, a look of terror on his face. Holmes hears that a large, mysterious hound has been intimidating and killing members of the Baskerville family for years. The dog's footprints have been spotted near Sir Charles's body. Holmes refuses to believe that a dog could cause so many deaths. With Dr. Watson's help, he discovers the truth.

Many countries boast Sherlock Holmes museums. These museums celebrate the life of Sherlock Holmes. The most famous of these is in London—at 221B Baker Street. The rooms of the museum look exactly like the rooms described in Doyle's stories. You can sit in an armchair by the fireplace—just as Holmes did— and have your photo taken. Or you can check out Holmes's famous hat, violin, magnifying glass, and chemistry set.

Sherlock Holmes is not just a detective. He is a legend. Sir Arthur Conan Doyle probably never imagined that his creation would live on so long. And Holmes will likely be around for years to come, solving the mysteries that stump everyone else.

The Sherlock Holmes Museum at 221B Baker Street in London

Practice the Skill

Literary Devices

1. Look at the section A Distinctive Detective. Fill in the chart below with two examples of figurative language used to describe Sherlock Holmes.

Figurative Language	Meaning	Type of Figurative Language
		Simile
		Metaphor

2. The text describes Dr. Watson as "Holmes's rock." What does this mean?

_____

_____

Check Comprehension

1. List two of Holmes's hobbies.

- _____

- _____

2. What two methods does Holmes use to solve crimes?

- _____

- _____

An Inspiring Investigator

1. Read the sentence below.

> **Clothes, fingerprints, and DNA speak loudly to investigators.**

What type of literary device is used? _____

What does the sentence mean? _____

_____

2. Write an example of alliteration from the text.

_____

Vocabulary

1. Use context clues to explain what *eccentric* means on page 71.

_____

2. Find the word *obsession* on page 72. Write a sentence using this word.

_____

_____

Writing

Reread the description of Sherlock Holmes on pages 70 and 71. Write a short description of someone you know well. Use literary devices in your description.

Text Connections

Now that you have read several mysteries, choose one of the following activities to investigate.

○ In a small group, brainstorm ideas for a campfire tale. Work together to write the story. Use a variety of literary devices to make it spooky.

○ Find a book of poetry in the library. Read the poems, and look for the literary devices. Make a list of the ones you like.

○ Work in pairs to write a short play about a problem at school. Use literary devices to make the dialogue more interesting.

○ Kyle accused his friends of stealing. Write an apology from Kyle to his friends, and ask for their forgiveness.

○ Imagine you are a detective who has stumbled across something suspicious. Write a short story in which you solve the crime.

○ Go to the Sherlock Holmes museum online (**http://www.sherlock-holmes.co.uk/home. htm**), and take the museum tour. Make a list of five new things you learned about Sherlock Holmes.

Continue your explorations by reading these books:

Two-Minute Mysteries by Donald J. Sobol
Dr. Haledjian can solve a mystery with just a handful of clues. Can you?

South By Southeast by Anthony Horowitz
The Diamond brothers are private investigators who find a dead body in a phone booth. Will they be next?

The Westing Game by Ellen Raskin
The winner could inherit Samuel Westing's millions of dollars. Can anyone solve the riddle?

DISASTER!

The Great Chicago Fire consumed the city, destroying everything in its path. Why was the fire so destructive?

Tom is separated from his family during the fire. Will his family survive?

In a city destroyed by fire, people are eager to place blame. But whose fault is it?

Unit 5

Recognizing Viewpoint: Author's Perspective Identify the background and beliefs of the author and then see how they influence the text.

CHICAGO POST

Wednesday, October 11, 1871

Fire in Chicago!

> *What different perspectives are expressed in this article?*

By Albert Trumble

A great fire burned Chicago to the ground over the past three days. The blaze is thought to have been started on Sunday night by a small, accidental fire on Chicago's West Side. Very dry conditions and strong winds combined to spread the fire throughout the city. Hundreds of people have died and thousands more have lost their homes. It could be weeks—even months—before we know for sure just how much damage has been done.

The Cause of the Fire

The Chicago Fire Department was first alerted to the fire at 10:00 p.m. on Sunday, October 8, when they received a report that the barn at the O'Leary property on DeKoven Street was on fire. A neighbor said, "Those O'Learys are the cause of this! They left a lantern in the barn and a cow kicked it over." This has not yet been confirmed.

Large fires are nothing new to the Chicago Fire Department. In fact, the city's firemen spent Saturday night putting out a huge blaze less than a mile from the O'Leary's. The 185 firemen worked through the night and into Sunday morning to put out the fire, and they were able to contain the blaze to just four blocks. They were still exhausted by the events of the first fire when they got word of Sunday's fire.

There was very little the firemen could do to contain Sunday's fire. Strong, twenty-mile-per-hour winds swept the blaze to other parts of the city. Dry conditions also contributed to the disaster—a lack of rainfall over the last few weeks made the city dry and very prone to fire.

Many people fled the city.

The Fire Spreads

Before the fire department could get to the O'Leary property, winds had pushed the flames northeast toward an industrial zone. "This whole area was a fire hazard," said one witness. "Wooden warehouses and sheds were full of dry goods and mountains of coal—everything that was there could burn! Why hadn't city officials realized that and taken action?" The officials could not be reached for comment.

The winds swept sparks from the fire farther northeast and across the river, causing the blaze to reach the more heavily populated areas of the city.

By midnight, the fire had roared through Conley's Patch, an Irish immigrant district of small, flimsy houses. Many people died there, trapped in their homes. "Building regulations have been ignored in this area," a fireman said. "Landlords were making big money on these shacks—and now people have died!"

The fire also caused a huge gas tank to explode, adding fuel to the already powerful flames. The power in the city then failed, making the fire the only light in the entire city.

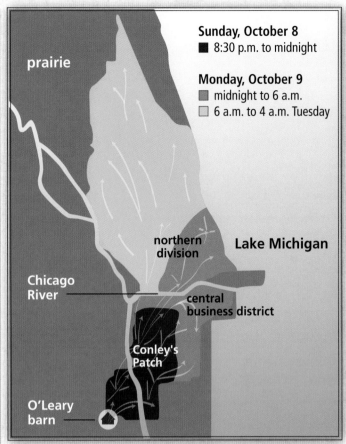

Sunday, October 8
■ 8:30 p.m. to midnight

Monday, October 9
■ midnight to 6 a.m.
□ 6 a.m. to 4 a.m. Tuesday

prairie

northern division

Lake Michigan

Chicago River

central business district

Conley's Patch

O'Leary barn

How the fire spread across Chicago

This made it harder for the firemen to do their job—and harder for residents to escape.

After midnight, the fire swept north into Chicago's central business district, and swirling winds made the fire even worse. "The wind was sucked into the center of the flames," said weather forecaster Thomas Mosher Jr. Winds pushed the flames into the air, causing a firestorm. It looked like the sky was on fire. "People are blaming the firemen," Mosher later added. "But no one could have controlled this."

After the firestorm, the fire continued to spread. Flaming debris flew through the air, and asphalt roofs bubbled and melted. The heat was so intense that buildings burst into flames before the fire could even touch them. Even buildings of brick and stone were destroyed, their walls crumbling from the extreme temperatures. Around 3:00 a.m., the fire destroyed the city's water works. Without water to put out the flames, all hope of saving the city vanished.

These men look at their ruined city.

The Fire Dies

On the morning of October 9, the fire headed farther into the northern division of the city, where thousands of German and Scandinavian immigrants lived. Many were still in bed, never expecting that the fire would reach them. Lives were lost, but fewer died here than in the area south of the river.

With help from a Monday night rainfall, the fire began to die out around midnight. By that time it had reached the prairie on the northernmost edge of the city. The blaze lasted for more than twenty-four hours and had reduced almost every building in its path to ashes.

It is still uncertain what will become of the thousands of people left homeless by the fire. Many people fled east to Lake Michigan, while others fled north to escape the blaze. Residents continue to return to the burned wreckage in hopes of reuniting with loved ones.

The future of Chicago remains uncertain. Many of its now-homeless residents are still coming to grips with this tragedy, while others are already talking about rebuilding. It could take several years before the city of Chicago is returned to its once-vibrant state. ❋

Practice the Skill

Recognizing Viewpoint: Author's Perspective

1. Read the first paragraph of The Cause of the Fire. What is the perspective of the neighbor?

   _____

   _____

2. Read the first paragraph of The Fire Spreads. What is the perspective of the witness?

   _____

   _____

3. What is Albert Trumble's perspective? Why is this his perspective?

   _____

   _____

Check Comprehension

List three reasons the fire was so destructive.

- _____

- _____

- _____

Vocabulary

Use each word in a sentence that shows its meaning.

- immigrant (page 79) _____

   _____

- debris (page 80) _____

   _____

Journal of Thomas Keating, Aged Fourteen

Monday morning, October 9, 1871

What are Tom's feelings throughout the disaster?

I have had bad nights before, but last night was by far the worst night of my life. As I write this, I am stranded on a distant lakeshore, alone except for my little sister, Clara. I don't know if my parents are alive or if our house still stands, and I have never been more afraid in my life.

It was less than twenty-four hours ago, but it seems like forever since Sunday night. It all started when Pa tore into my room and shook me awake. "Get up and dress quickly!" he cried. "A fire is only a few streets away and will be here in minutes!" I didn't believe him at first, but I jumped in surprise when I looked out the window. The sky was a smoky red, and the wind was blowing hard, pushing the flames directly toward our house.

I pulled on a coat over my nightshirt and looked for something important to save, until finally I grabbed my journal and baseball bat and ran downstairs. Ma and Clara were already at the door, Clara holding her two dolls, and Ma holding her canary in its cage.

"Tom, take Ma and Clara down to the lakeshore as fast as you can," Pa said.

"What about you, Charles?" Ma cried desperately. We all knew Pa was going to run to his office to try and save his business papers. "We should stay together!" Ma insisted.

Just then we heard a roaring sound, and a pine tree at the end of our street burst into flames and began burning like a torch—it seemed like the fire was alive. Clara began to cry, and I didn't think we would escape.

Clara was too afraid to move, so I grabbed her hand tightly and pulled her outside. Ma followed, but Pa headed off in the other direction without seeing which way we went. Once we were outside, we were sucked into a river of people all running toward the lake. With every step I was pushed, jostled, and shoved aside, as people dragged boxes, pulled carts, and pushed wheelbarrows loaded with their belongings.

I lost my grip on Clara's hand when a man pushed between us and shouted, "Get out of my way!" He didn't care that he'd just pushed over a little girl. I dropped my bat and picked Clara up.

That's when I noticed Ma was no longer behind us.

"Ma!" I shouted, but my voice was drowned out by the noise. I looked up and flames filled the sky. The heat was unbearable—as if the fire was trying to consume us.

"Where's Ma? Where's Ma?" I heard Clara cry frantically.

"We'll find her at the lake!" I replied as calmly as I could.

The roar of the fire got louder and louder as we raced toward the lake. People ran faster and started to throw away the things they'd been trying to save. We kept falling over people's abandoned belongings, and at one point I heard a man shout urgently to his wife, "The blankets don't matter anymore! Just drop them and run!"

At last we arrived at the lake, and there were hundreds of people there. No one knew what to do because there was no place to go. As I watched a few people pushing boats out onto the lake, I heard someone yell my name.

"Tom Keating!" It was a friend of my father's, Mr. Brennan, who was in a rowboat with his family. "We can take two more, so get in!"

"I can't find Ma!" I shouted.

"Get in now!" said Mr. Brennan. Without thinking, I threw Clara into the boat and climbed in after her, and at once, Mr. Brennan pushed off.

We could only sit and watch as the fire roared toward the lake. Clara covered her face with her hands, but I couldn't stop staring.

The fire died out when it reached the short grass at the edge of the lake. The people on shore waded into the water and splashed water over their faces and clothes.

Mr. Brennan rowed north where it was safer, and I helped him pull the boat onto the shore, where we are all now waiting for morning.

Tuesday evening, October 10, 1871

Oh, what a difference a day makes! I can barely contain my excitement, but I will try to write down what happened.

Yesterday was a sad and terrible day. Last night, I looked south toward the city and saw it was still on fire, but this morning I woke up and the fire had finally stopped! I told Mr. Brennan I must go look for Ma, and he kindly rowed Clara and me back.

There were a lot of people still sitting at the edge of the lake. I ran up and down the shore, looking at every face as Clara called for our mother. I was so afraid we would never see Ma again.

Then we found her!

She was sitting by the water, still holding the canary in its cage. She held her arms out, and we all clung together. I thought I was too old for hugs, but I found out I wasn't at all.

Ma said she hadn't seen Pa, but she thought that if we walked toward his office, we might find him. We knew that our house must be gone because all the streets around it had been destroyed.

It was hard to find our way to Pa's office, since everything looked different with most of the buildings gone.

When we reached Pa's office, a police officer stopped us, refusing to let us in the unsafe buildings.

We were dismayed and weren't sure where else Pa could be—or if he was even still alive. I felt empty inside and sick.

And then . . . we heard Pa's voice!

"Thank goodness I found you!" he cried. We turned around and saw Pa running toward us shouting, "Is everyone all right?" He'd been looking for us all day. "I knew you'd come back this way, if you were still . . ." He stopped, but we knew what he was thinking.

So, as I write this, we have no home, no belongings, and our father has no place to work. It has been the most terrible time of my life, yet I can't help but feel like everything will be okay. We've found each other, and that's all that matters.

Practice the Skill

Recognizing Viewpoint: Author's Perspective

Read the journal entry from Monday, October 9. Read the reasons below that support Tom's perspective. Then write his perspective in the box.

Tom's Perspective	_____ _____ _____
Reasons	• Tom has no idea if his parents are alive. • Tom has no idea if his house is still standing. • Tom is stranded on a distant lakeshore.

Check Comprehension

1. Why did Pa go in a different direction from the rest of the family?

   _____

   _____

2. Why did people leave their belongings in the middle of the road?

   _____

   _____

What a Difference a Day Makes

Tom has a different perspective on Tuesday, October 10. Write his new perspective below. Then write two reasons or examples that support it.

Tom's New Perspective

Reasons	

Vocabulary

1. Find *unbearable* on page 83. Write a sentence using this word.

   _____

   _____

2. On page 83, what does the phrase "the fire was trying to consume us" mean?

   _____

3. Write a word from page 85 that means "upset and uncertain."

   _____

Writing

Write a journal entry about the fire from the perspective of Tom's mother.

CHICAGO ✶ POST

Wednesday, November 8, 1871

The Great Fire: Who's to Blame?

> *What is Chief Artley's perspective on the disaster?*

By Joseph Morgan

It has been one month since the destruction of our city. The Great Fire of Chicago, as it is being called, is one of the worst disasters this nation has ever seen. Now, as residents work to restore what has been lost, people are asking questions. How could this happen, and why was the destruction so complete? Why couldn't our fire department stop, or at least contain, the blaze?

I decided to ask Fire Chief Jon Artley those very questions, and after our interview, I came away with a very different point of view. What follows are the questions I put to him, along with his replies.

━━━◆═❂═◆━━━

MORGAN: Sir, could your department have done more to stop the fire? If you had sent more firemen out when the fire first started, would fewer lives and less property have been lost?

CHIEF ARTLEY: There are two things I must say. First, I do not have, and have not had, as many firemen as I would like or need. I have said repeatedly that the fire department is seriously understaffed, but no action has been taken, and now we see the results.

Second, on the night the fire broke out, my men had had only a few hours sleep. We had gotten a call the previous night about a fire on the West Side. My men did an excellent job putting it out, but they were tired the next day. If I had more firemen under my command, there would have been fresh, rested firemen ready to go.

MORGAN: So you are saying your men did not respond quickly to the alarm raised on October 8 because they were tired?

CHIEF ARTLEY: No, I am not saying that at all! My men *did* respond quickly and worked well *even though* they were tired.

Fire Chief Artley

MORGAN: If your men worked well, then how did the fire spread so quickly?

CHIEF ARTLEY: You must remember we'd had no heavy rain since early July, which has made the city very dry. Apart from the center of the city, which was built of stone and brick, most of the city's buildings were made of wood—dry wood and fire is not a good combination.

There was also a strong wind that night, so as soon as the fire began, the wind pushed it along. It would not have mattered how many men were working because by then, the fire was out of control.

MORGAN: You say the buildings in the center of the city were made of stone and brick, and yet these buildings were also destroyed.

CHIEF ARTLEY: Yes, you certainly wouldn't expect buildings of stone and brick to burn, but think about what types of buildings they were: shops, warehouses, and storage areas, each one stacked from floor to ceiling with clothes, books, and other items that burn easily.

Plus, even though the walls were made of stone and brick, many buildings had decorative fronts made of wood, and others had flat roofs covered with highly flammable tarpaper. Some of my men told me they saw fire catching the roofs of these buildings. The flames entered the buildings through the roof and burned everything inside.

MORGAN: We've talked about the buildings, but what about the people? At least three hundred are dead. Couldn't your firemen have devoted their time to warning people, or helping them escape?

CHIEF ARTLEY: That's exactly what they did! After we realized the fire couldn't be contained, we put all our efforts into warning and rescuing people. I have already stated that the department is seriously understaffed, and if we had more firemen, we could have reached more people. My men did *everything* they could.

MORGAN: Surely they could have done *something* more!

CHIEF ARTLEY: I don't see how. My men told me of the panic in the streets and of people wandering half-blind through darkness and smoke. They told me of livestock loose and frantic in the crowd, and of families getting separated. It would have been impossible to warn or rescue everyone in a situation like that.

My men entered houses that were on the verge of bursting into flames to see whether anyone was still inside.

Sometimes they had to drag occupants out by force when people were too afraid to move. They carried children, the elderly, and the sick to safety, and they persuaded people to abandon their carts of household goods in order to save themselves. And you would sit here and suggest that they weren't doing enough?

A fireman rescues an infant.

MORGAN: I meant no criticism of the firemen, sir.

CHIEF ARTLEY: No criticism *should* be directed at them! They are heroes and should be congratulated, not questioned. And remember, too, some of them have also lost their homes or members of their families.

MORGAN: You are absolutely correct, sir, and I apologize. Thank you for your time.

✦━┅═◈═┅━✦

Exterior walls are all that remain of many buildings.

After my interview with Fire Chief Artley, I am convinced that the fire department is not to blame for the disaster. Now that we have an opportunity to rethink, rebuild, and replace, I believe there are lessons to be learned.

There are several things we must do. We need to pay attention to Fire Chief Artley's words and provide the fire department with more firemen, and we also need to improve our city planning. Too many weak buildings were crowded together in a small area. As we make plans for our new city, we have to make sure this does not happen again.

Fire prevention awareness must also be raised, and the storing of highly flammable articles in city buildings cannot continue.

I now realize that there isn't a single person, event, or condition to blame for this disaster. The weather could not have been controlled, and the city had been vulnerable to fires for a long time. A disaster like this was bound to happen, so this is not the time to be blaming anyone. We now have a chance to rebuild, and trying to place blame will not help us do that. The Great Fire has been a warning. We cannot, and we must not, let such an event occur again. ✳

Practice the Skill

Recognizing Viewpoint: Author's Perspective

Joseph Morgan had a specific perspective when he started the interview. Write his perspective and three reasons or examples that support it.

Morgan's Perspective	_____ _____
Reasons	• _____ _____ • _____ _____ • _____ _____

Check Comprehension

1. Write two reasons the stone and brick buildings burned so badly.

   • _____

   • _____

2. Write two reasons the firemen couldn't do any more to get the people out of danger.

   • _____

   • _____

Fearless Firemen

By the end of the interview, Joseph Morgan had changed his perspective. Write his changed perspective and two reasons or examples that support it.

Morgan's Changed Perspective
_____   _____

Reasons	
_____ _____ _____ _____ _____	_____ _____ _____ _____ _____

Vocabulary

1. Write the meanings of these words.

   - understaffed (page 88) _____

   - flammable (page 89) _____

   - livestock (page 90) _____

2. Write the sentence from page 91 that suggests what *vulnerable* means.

   _____

   _____

Writing

Imagine you are a reporter for the *Chicago Post*. Write an interview with a city official about the fire and its effects.

Text Connections

Now that you have read some texts about the Chicago Fire, explore the following topics.

- Research what happened after the Great Chicago Fire of 1871. What happened to people who lost their homes? How was the city rebuilt?

- What possessions would you save if you had to flee your home? Give reasons for your answers. Discuss your response with a partner.

- What do you think the O'Learys had to say about the fire? Write a paragraph from Mrs. O'Leary's perspective.

- Find a newspaper article that describes a disaster such as the 1980 eruption of Mount St. Helen or the Indian Ocean Tsunami of 2004. Imagine you survived the disaster, and write a journal entry to describe the story of your survival.

- Fold a piece of paper in half. Write "For" at the top of one half and "Against" at the top of the other. As a group, list arguments for and against a statement such as "In a disaster, rescue workers should always save pets—even if it means they have less time to save people." Present your group's arguments to the class and let the class vote on the strongest arguments.

Continue your explorations by reading these books:

The Exxon Valdez 1989: An Oil Tanker Runs Aground by John Townsend
The Exxon Valdez oil spill was one of the worst environmental disasters of all time. But how did it happen?

Fever 1793 by Laurie Halse Anderson
Yellow fever breaks out in Philadelphia and everyone is getting sick. Will Mattie get the disease, too?

World's Afire by Paul B. Janeczko
How does a fun day at the circus become one of America's worst disasters?

Intriguing Investigations

- Smallpox was a deadly disease, but one doctor found a way to prevent it. What did he risk to prove he was right?

- A class finds deformed frogs in the woods. What is causing this to happen?

- Two hikers stumble across some men digging holes in the desert sand. What are the men looking for?

Unit
6

Synthesizing Information   To synthesize information, combine information from several sources to draw your own conclusions.

A Risky Experiment

Why was smallpox such a dangerous disease?

In 1796, Dr. Edward Jenner made a small scratch in a little boy's arm and gave him the deadly smallpox disease on purpose. Jenner's experiment was very risky—if his theory was correct, he would be celebrated, but if not, he could be prosecuted.

The Symptoms

Smallpox is highly contagious—it can be very easily caught. At first, a person with smallpox develops a high fever and generally feels sick. Several days later a rash of small red spots appears, usually on the face, hands, and feet. The rash spreads quickly all over the body.

A few days later, the red spots turn into blisters filled with liquid, and after another week, the blisters develop scabs. As the scabs heal, the fever begins to go down, but the scabs often leave deep scars. Much worse, some people go blind from the disease, and many do not survive at all.

Many Native Americans died from smallpox.

The History

Historians believe smallpox first appeared in India or Egypt 3,000 years ago. Scientists even believe that the ancient Egyptian Pharaoh Ramses V had smallpox. The marks on his mummified remains could be smallpox scars.

Smallpox came to the New World with the European colonists. Native Americans had never been exposed to the disease before, and as a result, a smallpox epidemic swept across North America between 1775 and 1782. The disease nearly wiped out whole tribes of Native Americans.

By the late 1700s, scientists still had not found an effective way to treat smallpox. Children were especially at risk of catching and dying from the disease.

Children at Risk

In the 1700s, ten percent of the children born in Sweden and France died from smallpox.

The Idea

Dr. Edward Jenner had a medical practice in Gloucestershire (GLOS-ter-sher), a region in southwest England. Many of his patients were farmers who got a disease called cowpox from their cows. Cowpox was similar to smallpox, but not as deadly. When a smallpox epidemic came to Gloucestershire in 1788, Jenner noticed that the people he had treated for cowpox did not catch smallpox.

Jenner began to think that he might give people cowpox to keep them from getting smallpox. But should he *give* someone a disease? What if something went wrong and his patient died?

Jenner decided to try. A milkmaid came to him with blister-like sores on her hands. Jenner knew that she had cowpox, so he drew out some liquid from her cowpox blisters. At the same time, Jenner had a patient with a mild case of smallpox, so he drew out some liquid from the smallpox blisters as well.

Then all Jenner needed was a healthy person to test his idea on. He explained the idea to a local farmer and asked if he could test it on the farmer's eight-year-old son, James. Jenner told the farmer that the boy would catch cowpox and then be exposed to smallpox. It was a risky thing to do, but the farmer decided it was worth it.

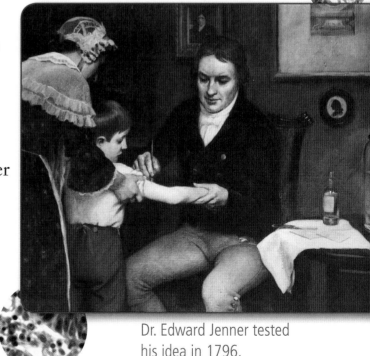

Dr. Edward Jenner tested his idea in 1796.

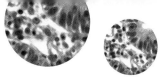

The Experiment

Jenner scratched James's arm and then put the liquid from the cowpox blisters into the cut. James did develop cowpox, but he was healthy again in about six weeks. Then Jenner scratched James's arm again, only this time, he put the liquid from the smallpox blisters into the cut. Jenner's experiment was a success—James did not catch smallpox.

Jenner wrote a report about his research, calling this process a *vaccine*, which comes from Latin for "of cows." Many people thought the idea was ridiculous, but by 1800, doctors found that vaccination worked, and many began to use it on their patients.

The Campaign

Smallpox may have had a vaccine, but it didn't disappear overnight. In the early 1900s, the disease continued to infect people all over the world. The World Health Organization (WHO) started a worldwide campaign to get rid of smallpox in the early 1950s. The last case of smallpox was reported about twenty years later.

How Does Vaccination Work?

1. A person is injected with microorganisms (like bacteria or a virus) that cause a disease. They are injected with only a mild dose of the disease.

2. The person's body produces antibodies, special substances that fight the disease. The antibodies stay in the person's body to protect it from the disease.

3. When the person is exposed to the full disease, the antibodies are already there. The antibodies can fight the disease more easily.

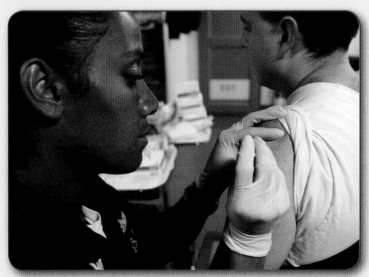

People are still vaccinated against various diseases.

Practice the Skill

Synthesizing Information

Draw a conclusion to answer the question. Use information from the text and the graphic on page 97 to support your conclusion.

Why did the farmer agree to Jenner's plan?

Conclusion

_____

_____

_____

Information

• It was a risky thing to do, but the farmer decided it was worth it.

• _____

_____

• _____

_____

Check Comprehension

How does injecting people with a small dose of smallpox keep them from getting the full disease?

_____

_____

Vocabulary

What does *epidemic* mean?

_____

What are some reasons frogs might be in danger?

The Case of the Deformed Frogs
BY TERESA MARTINEZ

In 1995, science teacher Cindy Reinitz and her students were headed toward the woods near their school in Henderson, Minnesota. They weren't looking for anything special. Reinitz just wanted her students to have an opportunity to appreciate the area they lived in. But when they stopped to look at a pond full of frogs, they noticed something unusual. One of the frogs had a back leg that was very, very thin. Then they spotted a frog that was missing a back leg altogether. The students started to look more closely. They caught twenty-two frogs and discovered that half of them were deformed. Normally, only about 1 in 10,000 animals of a species is deformed.

The students put three of the deformed frogs in a bucket. When they got back to the school, Reinitz called the Minnesota Pollution Control Agency. When the scientists saw the frogs, they could hardly believe their eyes.

Henderson wasn't the only place where deformed frogs were found. Before long, reports of deformed frogs were coming in from all over Minnesota and from other states as well. According to the 2001 Legislative Fact Sheet of the Minnesota Pollution Control Agency, scientists in Hibbing, Minnesota, found that "sixty-eight percent of frogs at the site were malformed."

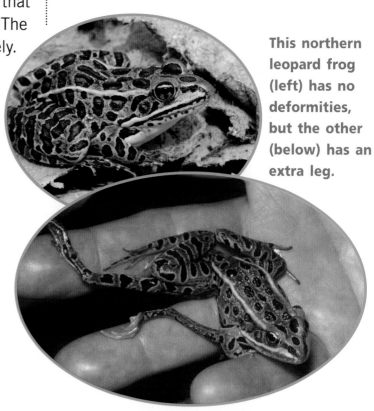

This northern leopard frog (left) has no deformities, but the other (below) has an extra leg.

FROG FACTS

- Water is very important to the frog life cycle. Frogs spend their early life in pools of water, first as eggs, and later as tadpoles. They also need water to grow to adulthood and to breed. When frogs reach adulthood, they move onto land.

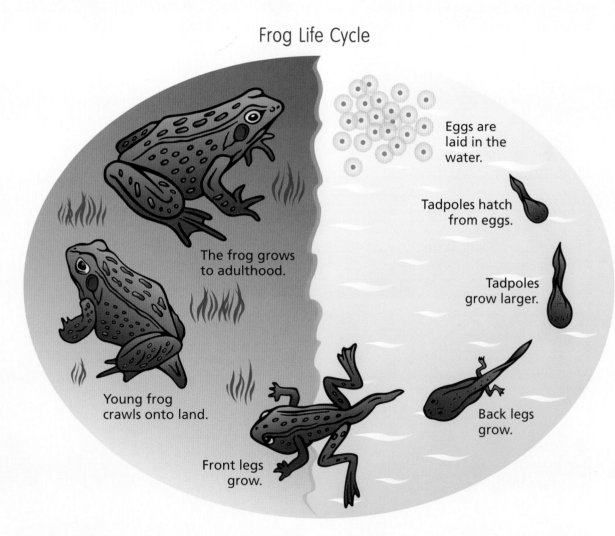

Frog Life Cycle

Eggs are laid in the water.

Tadpoles hatch from eggs.

Tadpoles grow larger.

Back legs grow.

Front legs grow.

The frog grows to adulthood.

Young frog crawls onto land.

- Frogs have very sensitive skin. Their skin absorbs almost everything they need, including water, minerals, and oxygen. Frog skin can also absorb harmful substances from air and water. An increase in harmful substances too small to affect mammals and birds may greatly affect frogs.

A Scientific Mystery

Over the last forty years, scientists have noticed that numbers of amphibians (including frogs, toads, and salamanders) are decreasing worldwide. There are about 6,000 species of amphibians in the world, and many of them are dying out. Frogs seem to be in the most danger. Some species of frogs have completely disappeared from areas where they once lived. Other species may become extinct very soon. Among some species there is a large number of deformed frogs. Scientists have identified six reasons for the disappearing and deformed frogs.

Each of these reasons gives scientists clues, but none gives them a clear answer. The mystery is not yet solved, but scientists are still at work. Hopefully they will find the answer soon—while there is still time.

A frog's skin is very sensitive and can absorb dangerous substances.

Habitat Destruction Cutting trees and draining marshes are just two of the reasons frogs are losing more and more of their land and water habitats.

Climate Change Frogs react very quickly to small changes in temperature. Frogs' bodies may have trouble adjusting to higher air and water temperatures. A change in temperature may be too much for their bodies to handle.

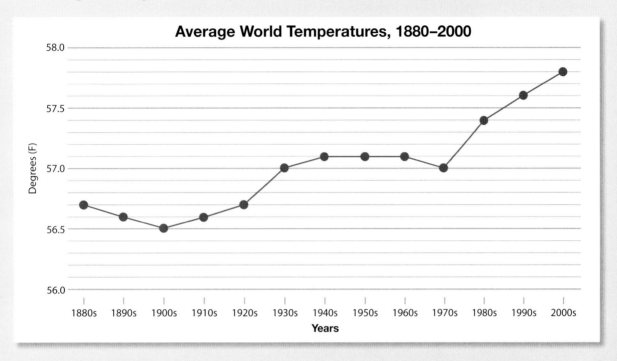

Pollution Frogs living near farming areas are especially at risk. Some farmers use artificial fertilizers and weed killers to help crops grow. Some also use pesticides to control insects. These chemicals can cause deformities or even death in frogs.

Disease Scientists in Australia found frogs with an unusual skin disease. They found out that a fungus caused the disease. Soon, frogs with this skin disease started appearing in other parts of the world. Usually, this type of fungus is harmless. Something else—in combination with the fungus—may have affected the frogs.

Atmosphere There are high levels of ultraviolet radiation in the atmosphere today. It may be too strong for frogs to survive.

New Species When new species are introduced into frog habitats, frog species are challenged. For example, some frogs die out when humans introduce fish into their habitats. Why? Many frogs must lay their eggs in water that is free of fish. When humans take over a pond and fill it with fish, the fish may eat the frogs' eggs.

Practice the Skill

Synthesizing Information

Draw a conclusion to answer the question. Use information from page 100 and the first paragraph on page 102 to support your conclusion.

Are frogs doing well or are they in trouble?

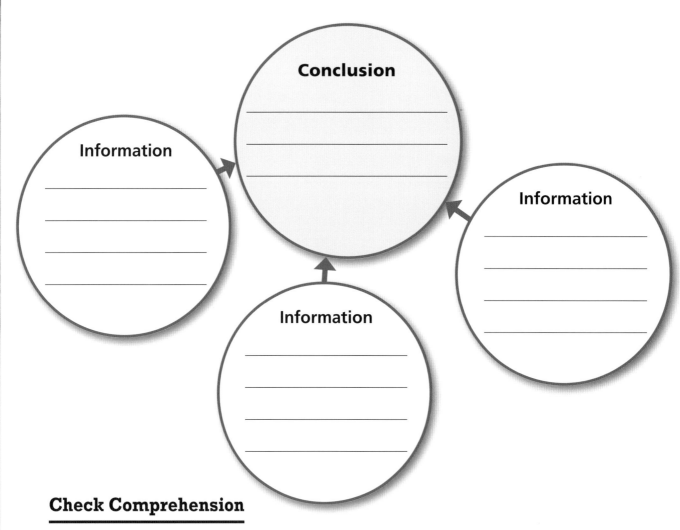

Check Comprehension

1. Why did Cindy Reinitz and her students go into the woods?

   _____

   _____

2. Who did Cindy Reinitz call about the frogs?

   _____

Frog Logic

1. How do the Frog Facts on page 101 help you understand the list of reasons on page 103? Give two examples.

   - _____

   - _____

2. Look at the graph on page 103. What does it suggest about the earth's temperature?

   _____

   How might this affect frogs?

   _____

   _____

Vocabulary

1. Write the sentence from page 102 that tells what *extinct* means.

   _____

   _____

2. Write a word from page 103 that means "the natural environment of an animal or plant."

   _____

Writing

What do you think is the major reason frogs are becoming deformed or dying? Explain your reasoning.

Last Man's Gorge

How did Amy and Glen know the men they saw were thieves?

SUMMER IN NEW MEXICO IS HOT, BUT GLEN DOESN'T CARE. HE AND HIS SISTER AMY ARE HEADING FOR THE MUSEUM OF NATIVE AMERICAN ARTIFACTS JUST PAST LAST MAN'S GORGE.

We're lost! I knew we should have asked someone for directions.

We're not lost. We've only been walking an hour and a half! We're almost there.

We're right about here, and the museum is just beyond the gorge.

We'll have to hurry if we want to make it to the museum before it closes.

Hey, what's going on by those ruins?

What are those guys doing?

I don't know.

AMY ZOOMS IN TO GET A CLOSER LOOK.

GLEN AND AMY DESCRIBE TO THE MUSEUM WORKER WHAT THEY SAW.

SERGEANT NORANJO ARRIVES AT THE MUSEUM A FEW HOURS LATER.

Practice the Skill

Synthesizing Information

Draw a conclusion to answer the question. Use information from page 107 to support your conclusion.

What were the men doing in Last Man's Gorge?

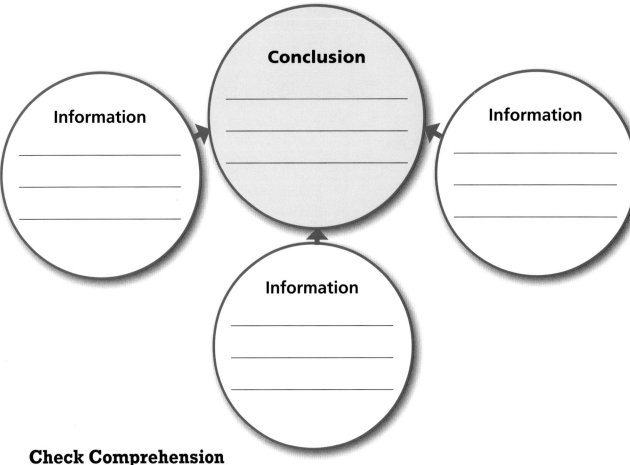

Check Comprehension

1. Why did Glen tell Amy they would have to hurry while they were hiking?

   _____

   _____

2. What does Amy look at when she first arrives at the museum? What does Glen look at?

   _____

   _____